CONFESSIONS OF A FORMER DITTOHEAD

•

Jim Derych

Brooklyn, New York

Ig Publishing
178 Clinton Avenue
Brooklyn, NY 11205

www.igpub.com

Library of Congress Cataloging-in-Publication Data

Derych, Jim.
  Confessions of a former dittohead / Jim Derych.
    p. cm.
  Includes bibliographical references (p.   ).
  ISBN-13: 978-0-9752517-8-2
  ISBN-10: 0-9752517-8-3
  1. Conservatism—United States. 2. Derych, Jim. 3. Limbaugh, Rush H. 4.
Republican Party (U.S. : 1854-) 5. United States—Politics and government—
1989-1993. 6. United States—Politics and government—1993-2001. 7. United
States—Politics and government—2001- I. Title.
  JC573.2.U6D47 2006
  320.52092—dc22
                            2005036452

ISBN-10: 0-9752517-8-3
ISBN-13: 978-0-9752517-8-2

CONTENTS

•

PART II: THE DITTOHEAD BRAIN

ACKNOWLEDGEMENTS

•

You will read much in these pages about my transformation from "dittohead," or "larval-stage human being," into the majestic progressive butterfly that flits before you on these pages. There are many people who helped make this transformation possible. But there's one person who deserves a lot of the credit for putting up with a dittohead for the better part of the last decade: my wife Becky. Here's to spending the rest of my life on the same side of the fence as the person I love.

There are others whose arm-twisting, cajoling, and occasional outright activism were critical to getting this book written and published. A great deal of credit goes to my mom for aggressively encouraging what has become a lifelong love of reading. And you can't very well thank your mom without also thanking your dad. I have to thank him for turning me on to Rush Limbaugh in the first place. After reading this book you may think that I have a bad opinion of my dad; I hope that isn't the case, because in truth my dad has the biggest heart of any person I've ever known. Cynical and judgmental, maybe, but whose dad isn't cynical and judgmental? In many ways I can only hope to be half the man that he is today.

I also want to thank Markos Moulitsas Zúniga, founder of Daily Kos, for giving me a forum through which to vent, share ideas and ultimately write this book. I'd also like to thank the members of the Daily Kos community for their enthusiasm, particularly Heather Henderson, or "hrh" as she is known in the Kos community. Thanks also go to Ben Morrison, who pointed out my diaries to the fine folks over at Ig Publishing; Rebecca Mabry for allowing me to call upon her invaluable publishing experience for free; Scott Betts, who introduced me to Al Franken's political writings; my three cats, Crystal Ball, Tiger, and Fluffy for their constant moral support; and finally, Robert and Elizabeth with Ig Publishing for taking a chance on a "nonwriter."

INTRODUCTION

•

During the 2004 presidential election, web logs (or blogs) became all the rage. One that I frequently visited was Daily Kos, a progressive website run by Markos Moulitsas. Daily Kos usually had the latest poll results, as well as breaking news on issues like Abu Ghraib. For the latter half of 2004, I became what the blog community calls a "lurker," meaning I would read the stories, but wouldn't make any comments. After the election was over, however, I decided that I had to get some things off my chest. I had helped elect Bush the first time, and I wasn't very happy about it. I'd let Rush Limbaugh lie to me for 13 years, and I wanted to vent.

On February 1, 2005, I wrote my first diary for Daily Kos, entitled "Confessions of a Former Dittohead." It was short (348 words), and I was shocked at all the attention it got from the Kos community. I received nearly 300 comments from other readers wondering what had caused me to change my mind, and asking how they might get other dittoheads to see the light. I went on to write dozens of "Dittohead" diaries, some of which formed the foundation for this book.

Many liberals posted links to my diaries on conservative sites. That's when the hate mail started. Occasionally, however, a curious conservative would contact me to ask about my story and why I had gone from right to left. One such individual, after reading my diary on how tax cuts don't increase federal revenue, asked, "Do you really believe that?" It's not a matter of "believing it," I wrote back; it's a matter of accepting the truth. You have to be strong enough to admit that tax cuts don't result in more federal revenue. You need to be able to see the colossal failures of the Bush administration in Iraq and Afghanistan and demand some accountability for that. You have to be willing to hold the Republicans' feet to their own philosophical fire, because personal responsibility, the mantra of the Republicans, is meaningless if you're not willing to apply it to members of your own party.

Ultimately, I didn't so much leave the Republican Party as much as the Republican Party left me. It was the way they closed ranks around the president, even in the face of overwhelming evidence of gross negligence. It stopped being about governing, and evolved into just doing whatever it takes to stay in power. Don't like a scientific report? Change it! Want to give huge tax cuts to the top 1 percent, but still want to spend money like it's going out of style? Just do it! We'll blame 9/11! Running against a decorated war veteran? Call him an unpatriotic coward! Don't like what some former ambassador had to say about your Iraq policy? Out his CIA-agent wife, or blame the liberal media—

either one will work. Want to torture people? Knock yourself out! We'll just call it a fraternity prank; just do whatever you have to do to stay in power. Right and wrong? Those are concepts for the other side to worry about. As long as we keep saying we're right, then we're right!

In short, it was the complete abandonment of anything remotely resembling intellectual honesty that caused me to change sides. If the Republican Party of today doesn't sicken you, then you're not paying attention. I didn't pay attention for years, and looking back, all I have to say is, I got duped. But now's the time for that to change. I concluded my very first diary on Daily Kos with this paragraph:

I have no intended audience for this diary. I'm not trying to change anyone's mind about any particular issue. I just want to write about how I got to where I am today because it's cathartic, and I've got a lot of things that I'm sorry about.

I still don't have an intended audience, but maybe in the following pages you'll find something to change your mind. If you're a Democrat reading this, maybe you'll have a little more sympathy for the average dittohead lost in the political wilderness. If you're a dittohead, maybe you'll read something that will change your mind, or at least force you to look at things in a different light. Regardless, I feel a whole lot better putting my story down in words. And ever since I posted that first diary, I've greatly enjoyed doing things that I'm proud of!

PART I
FROM DITTOHEAD TO DEMOCRAT

1 : MY FIRST CONFESSION

•

It's high time I finally confront the chubby, drug-addicted, matrimonially challenged elephant that resides in the living room of my political past: Rush Limbaugh.

Hi, everyone. My name's Jim, and I'm a former dittohead.

For those of you who are unaware, a dittohead is a loud, judgmental, unapologetic listener of Rush Limbaugh. Being a dittohead means you think that Rush is the beginning, middle, and end of political knowledge and information, and that that knowledge and information always show that Republicans are right, liberals (and everyone else) wrong. Dittoheads believe "if only you understood politics, you'd be a Republican." Liberalism doesn't make sense to them. From abortion to gay marriage to national defense to fiscal policy, there is only the "Republican way." And, to them, no one articulates the "Republican way" more clearly than Rush Limbaugh.

Non-dittoheads think the term is derogatory, that it is someone who mindlessly parrots what Rush says. That's a common misconception. The term actually comes from the early days of Rush's show, when people would begin virtually every call with some variation of "I'm so glad you're on the radio. It's good to have someone on the air who represents our political views." That took up a lot of airtime. One day after a caller really let fly with the flowery praise, the next guy started his call by saying, "Hey Rush, what that guy just said? Ditto." And the term "dittohead" was born.

That's not to say there aren't people who do mindlessly parrot everything Rush says, who live entirely inside the closed circle of Rushspeak, who are so tired of what they perceive to be a liberal bias in the mainstream media that they have stopped getting their news from anyone but Rush. When you have crossed this line, you have ceased being a dittohead and become what I call a "dittiot."

I crossed that line. But I've crossed back.

Rush to Judgment

My first exposure to Rush came when I was 18 years old, in 1991, when my parents drove me from home, which was Germantown, Tennessee (just outside of Memphis), to my freshman year of college at the University of Tennessee—Knoxville. My father was a huge Rush fan, so I had no choice but to listen during the six-hour drive. Rush's three-hour show gets you halfway there (reflecting a constant theme of Rush, which is getting you halfway to an unsupported allegation and then letting you go the rest of the way on your own). After one listen, I was hooked.

Prior to listening to Rush, I had few, if any political opinions. The one opinion I did have related to the spread of AIDS. Because it's not an airborne disease, I believed that all we needed to do to stop the epidemic was to quarantine everyone who had HIV. Simple. Put them on an island like we did with the lepers, drop medicine via parachute to ease their suffering and let them die out. Hitler would have been proud of that logic. And, sadly, that was about as deep as my well of political opinion went.

I was the perfect target for Rush. Against his onslaught of "undeniable truths," I never had a chance. He spoke with such certainty and authority, and, back then, there wasn't an Al Franken or an Air America or a liberal blogosphere to debunk him. For three hours a day, every day, Rush became the only person whose political and social opinions I would listen to. He argued so passionately for the protection of the unborn that he convinced me to be pro-life. He loved the military so much that he didn't want to see their operational efficiency compromised by allowing gays in the military. (With my homophobic attitude, that one was an easy sell for me.) In his book *The Way Things Ought to Be*, Rush showed how Reagan's tax cuts resulted in more federal revenue. Therefore if the government raised taxes, the government would actually get less money. Democrats were just too stupid to understand this.

The way the world works is all so simple when you listen to Rush. Simply put, liberals believe X, where X equals the most extreme viewpoint expressed by the most left-leaning liberal. Conservatives believe Y, Y being the opposite of whatever X is. There's no need to go and find out if *most* liberals believe X. And even if you did try to verify it, where are you going to get the truth from? The liberal media?

Let me take you through an example of how the "Rush Way" works. Let's start with an issue like abortion. First, understand that the dittohead's opposition to abortion comes back to the conservative notion of "Personal Responsibility." Simply put, a woman who wants an abortion is trying to avoid taking personal responsibility for her actions. Therefore the very term "pro-choice" is a fallacy. The woman already made a choice. She made the choice to have sex. Now she's just trying to avoid the consequences of her actions.

Rush describes these women as "feminazis." In an effort to deflect criticism, Rush goes apoplectic when people use this word in the wrong way. The correct definition of a feminazi is someone who thinks all sex is rape and that every fetus should be aborted. The more you listen to Rush, and the more he drums his assertions into your head, the more you begin to think that all feminists are feminazis. Then you start to think that Democrats think sex is rape, and that they believe every fetus should be aborted. Then you start to hate all Democrats for their unreasonable beliefs. It really is that slippery a slope.

As a result of this logic, from the ages of 18 to 31, I was lost to the world, voting Bush-Quayle in '92 and Dole-Kemp in '96. I was such a knob that after the '92 election I flipped my Bush-Quayle sign over and made a homemade "Dole-Kemp '96" sign on the back, leaving it in my apartment window for a year and a half.

I cheered when the Supreme Court ruled in favor of Bush in 2000. I gloated to my best friend (who's a Democrat) when Max Cleland got voted out of office in 2002. I was deliriously happy when the Paul Wellstone funeral backfired on the Democrats. When I was in Boston in 2002, I flipped off war protesters (from the safety of my cab). "Those people just hate Bush!" I thought. "Who in their right mind would oppose the disarmament of Saddam Hussein when it's so obvious that he's got weapons of mass destruction?"

The Conservative Spectrum

So what led me to see the light? While the process of my transformation was gradual, the transformation itself was instant. My dittiotism died the death of a thousand cuts. But it wasn't until the day of the thousandth cut that I officially cut ties with the Republican Party. During the intervening years, I was working my way down the conservative spectrum. For those unfamiliar with the spectrum, here's what it looks like (right to left, of course):

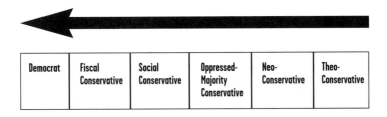

Democrat	Fiscal Conservative	Social Conservative	Oppressed-Majority Conservative	Neo-Conservative	Theo-Conservative

My starting point in college was as a **Theo-Conservative**, or **Theo-Con**. As a theo-con, you want official government recognition of your faith, God in public schools, homosexuals back in the closet, and all abortion to be considered murder. If the Ten Commandments were on display in schools and court-houses, we'd have less crime. Criminal behavior is just ignorance of God's laws. Sex shouldn't be taught at all, but if it is, it'd better be of the abstinence-only variety. Foreign policy? It's our God versus their god. We can fight any war we please; God won't abandon us. (It is in no small way ironic that the theo-con response to 9/11 has been to become more like the Taliban.) "Science is relative! Morals are absolute! Women should quit their jobs and homeschool! Screw civil liberties, as long as I'm safe!" Theo-cons want a government based on the Bible (but don't think the Sharia—Koranic law—should be the basis for Iraq's government).

The next step to the left is the **Neo-Conservative, or Neo-Con**. A neo-con is basically the same thing as a theo-con, but without all the Godspeak. They believe America has to project its power to protect itself. This is also known as the "Domino Theory of Democracy." Neo-cons' concerns are typically about 55 percent fiscal/foreign policy, 45 percent social. This mixing of conservative elements creates a sort of "worst of both worlds" Republican. Neo-cons are self-righteous and judgmental but lack the humility usually associated with being a "good Christian." They have contempt for those who fall through the cracks of society, because they believe the poor should take responsibility for themselves. The idea of a balanced budget is perceived as being quaint at best, and liberal at worst.

However, they also believe that the government has a lot to do in order to push their agenda. It has to make marriage and adoption for straights only, privatize Social Security, fight X number of foreign wars, subsidize farmers (yeah, that's a government handout, but remember, the Red States are mostly southern), and keep us safe domestically. Oh, and do all these things while simultaneously cutting taxes. Neo-cons believe in champagne government on a beer budget.

The **Oppressed-Majority Conservatives** are sort of like Diet Neo-Cons. From a policy perspective they have the same values set as the neo-con, but lack the neo-con's swagger. The oppressed-majority conservative is whiny and passive-aggressive. They respond to criticism by complaining that no one respects their views, even though their views are represented by majorities in all three branches of the government. Much like Montressor, they feel slighted, but the rest of us don't know why. Some feel as though they're being persecuted by the liberal media. Others are tired of the classroom atheist having the authority to keep Bible study out of the schools. As a whole, they feel like they are marginalized by society. You'd think the fact that their party controls the House, the Senate, the White House, and the Supreme Court might make them feel a bit more confident. But hey, why let facts get in the way of an otherwise perfectly good martyr complex?

Social Conservatives tend to be "limited-issue" conservatives. They may not always tow the party line, but if you run afoul of their big issue they will smack you down. They're pro-life, they don't want gay marriage, but they're not exactly thrilled to be at war with Iraq, and the budget deficit kind of bugs them. These are people of good conscience and consistent beliefs (e.g., against abortion and the death penalty).

The **Fiscal Conservative** has always been in favor of smaller government, lower taxes, and socially "whatever results in smaller government and lower taxes." Fiscal conservatives believe in the primacy of the private sector but understand that from time to time the government has to step in and stop things from getting out of control. The time of the fiscally conservative Republican is gone in modern politics. They've been marginalized in their own party and relegated to the status of "you're next once we get rid of the Democrats." For proof just ask your average dittohead friend what they think of Olympia Snow, Arlen Specter, and John McCain.

The one question I hear more than any other is "How can I convince my dittohead family/friends/coworkers that they live in a fantasy world?" Or to put it another way, how can you convert the average dittohead? Unfortunately, there is no easy answer to that question. You don't go from theo-con to Democrat in one night. Those to the right of the "social" and "fiscal" conservatives have a tremendous ability to dismiss information that doesn't agree with their worldview.

But there are only so many cuts a conservative belief system can endure. The best I can do is to tell my story. I can tell the tale of my thousand cuts, and maybe you can find things there to counter what you hear from your dittohead friends. As Mark Twain once said, "History doesn't repeat itself, but it does rhyme." You may not find an exact parallel, but maybe you'll find something that rhymes.

2 : WHAT'S WITH ALL THE HATE?

•

My childhood was far from what you might call typical. I was born in Miriam, Kansas, just outside of Kansas City, but my family moved almost immediately. Before I was 13 I had lived in Omaha, Nebraska; St. Louis, Missouri; Germantown, Tennessee; Dallas, Texas; Chicago, Illinois; Phoenix, Arizona; Monroe, Louisiana; Little Rock, Arkansas; and then back to Germantown.

"So," you may be inclined to ask, "was your family in the military?" Not unless you count fighting in the Cola Wars. My dad first worked for PepsiCo, then went to work for a Coke bottler in Phoenix, and finally a Pepsi bottler in the South.

For a child, moving around does have its advantages. You learn how to make friends quickly, you don't get too attached to anything, and you don't take yourself too seriously. But it has two major drawbacks—you're always the "new kid," and you're left with some serious insecurities. (Plus I was an only child, which means I had to face things by myself.) And, there is no more natural home for the insecure loner than Rush Limbaugh. Rush makes you feel like you're an insider. Like you get it and nobody else does. That you're not alone. That's how I got hooked.

My dad doesn't have that excuse. He had two siblings, lived in the same place growing up, and is about as self-confident a man as you're likely to meet. So how did Rush get him? Simply, just like Rush, my father was originally a Nixon Republican.

The first real political discussion I had with my dad was about Nixon. I was 11 years old at the time, and we were taking a road trip to New Orleans. Dad brought along a comedy tape by Nixon impersonator David Frye called *I Am the President . . . and Make No Mistake About That* to listen to on the drive. It was a lampoon of the Nixon administration (pre-Watergate) and featured skits such as Nixon trying pot, as well as bits making fun of an overly articulate Bill Buckley, the Apollo moon landings, and Henry Kissinger. Strange as it seems, my dad loved it, and I did too, even though I didn't understand much of the humor.

I vaguely remembered learning in school that Nixon "was fired or something," and I asked my dad what happened to him. The answer was simple: The liberal media wanted to bring down a conservative president, so they just hounded him until he quit. (For those on the liberal side of the political spectrum, you'll need a little background on the dittohead understanding of the liberal media. Like pornography, you can't exactly document the media's liberal bias, but you know it when you see it. That's why 2004's CBS "Memogate" was such a landmark story for conservatives. It offered for the first time concrete evidence of a liberal media bias.) Nixon did some questionable things, my dad agreed, but it wasn't anything that presidents before Nixon hadn't done. The media used to turn a blind eye to these activities, and the only reason they didn't do the same for Nixon was because he was a Republican. It was my first exposure to the concept of a liberal media, and it was kind of frightening. If the media can bring down the president, what else can they do?

The First One's Free, Kid

With those kinds of thoughts (and fears) already germinating inside of me, I was susceptible to a Rush onslaught, which occurred, as I mentioned before, on the day my parents drove me to college in 1991. Instead of listening to a Nixon comedy tape, this time my dad wanted to listen to this guy named Rush Limbaugh. My mom didn't know anything about Rush at the time, and when she asked who we were listening to, I responded, "Some hate-monger named Rush Limbaugh." I think that one of my friends used that phrase to describe Rush, and I never took the time to look into it. That lack of intellectual curiosity would serve me well as a dittohead.

"He's not a hate-monger!" my dad replied. "He's a harmless, lovable little fuzzball!" My mom and dad argued for a few minutes about what to listen to, as my mom wanted to hear the soundtrack from the 1958 film *Gigi*. (I couldn't win for losing that day.) Thankfully (or at least I thought so at the time), my dad, and Rush, won.

A Young Skull Full of Clinton-Hating Mush

As you can imagine, becoming a dittohead in the early 1990s meant that much of my early political life was consumed with a burning hatred of William Jefferson Blythe Clinton. What was it in particular about Clinton that drove me—and other ditto-heads—so buggy? And why were Congressional Republicans willing to drop everything just so they could put a figurative DNA stain on the equally figurative blue dress that is Clinton's legacy?

In the interest of full disclosure, my first impressions of Clinton were formed long before he ran for president. I lived in Little Rock from 1983 to 1985, when he was governor of Arkansas. Governor Clinton's sexual escapades were the stuff of rumors even in my sixth- and seventh-grade classrooms. (There wasn't a whole lot else to do in Arkansas besides eating at Shorty Smalls over on Rodney Parham, hitting the Putt-Putt by the interstate and gossiping about the Clintons.)

As a result, I laughed when I heard that Bill Clinton was going to run against George Sr. Not only did Bush have an approval rating in the low 90s, but he was a war hero; Clinton had avoided Vietnam. In addition, Clinton wouldn't answer questions about drug use in his past. It was, in short, a choice between a man who served his country with distinction and some yokel whose many indiscretions would easily keep him out of office. I sort of felt sorry for Bill. He had no chance.

Even though we dittoheads were upset when Clinton some-how won, we consoled ourselves with the fact that Clinton didn't get a majority of the popular vote. In fact, most people voted *against* Clinton, not for him. He had no mandate. (Didn't win the popular vote . . . no mandate. Sound familiar?)

If you were a Republican, you knew that there were two rea-sons why Clinton got elected. The first and biggest one: Bush raised taxes. By breaking that sacred trust with the Republican base, Bush allowed the creation of the second reason why Clinton won: Ross Perot. As a dittohead, you know that anytime you lose, it's not because of the issues. (Remember, "If people only *understood* politics, they'd be Republican.") The real answer to why Clinton won was because Bush did himself in, with help from Perot.

Early in his presidency, I actually didn't hate Clinton. I saw him being interviewed by Brokaw or Jennings in jeans the night before his inauguration, and I thought, "This guy's pretty cool." I felt like we'd be in pretty good hands, even though I disagreed with him politically.

Then came October 3, 1993. Dateline: Somalia. Eighteen U.S. Rangers dead, dozens wounded, the TV filled with images of our fallen soldiers being dragged through the streets. Logical people knew who to blame: Bush 41. Operation: Restore Hope was something he threw us into while he was running out the door in December of 1992, dropping 25,000 troops into a political nightmare with no clear definition of victory, no exit strategy and very little operational guidance as to what we were supposed to do. Clinton inherited a situation in which, if he stays, he's getting involved in a particularly messy civil war, but if he leaves, it looks like he doesn't care. What can he do? It's like the captain of the Titanic just handed him the hat and the wheel and said, "Good luck with this. Remember, whatever happens, it's your fault."

However, we dittoheads didn't blame Bush 41—we blamed Clinton. Clinton left those troops to die because he hated the military. He had to hate the military because he avoided serving in it. In fact, Democrats have always hated the military. Just like they did in Vietnam. As a dittohead, you believe that Democrats protested the Vietnam War because they hated the military, not because the war was unjust or was a waste of our time, money, resources, and most important, our blood. No, it was about Democrats hating the military and everything it stands for. I fully expect Ann Coulter to write a book someday about how we would have won the Vietnam War were it not for Democrats.

When I first started posting material on the internet, I would sign my messages with the following statement: "Politics—it's all fun and games until someone dies." With Clinton it was all fun and games until October 3, when, as a dittohead, you firmly believed he wanted the military to fail. And with a little prodding from Rush, it was a short journey to saying that Clinton wanted the troops to die.

After that, hating Clinton was a cakewalk—from Gennifer Flowers to Whitewater to commodities trading to Vince Foster to Paula Jones to Monica. Clinton was guilty of everything he'd been accused of, regardless of the facts. As a dittohead you know you couldn't get the facts even if you tried, since the liberal media wants to push its own agenda, not give you the facts.

Case in point: Vince Foster. As late as the 2004 election, here's what I believed about the Foster suicide: Vince was having an affair with Hillary, wrote a suicide note giving a full confession, then killed himself in his office. He was discovered not in his office, but in a park across the street. The suicide note was never found.

Here's reality: The day before he killed himself, Vince Foster called his doctor about depression. Foster shot himself in the head, and was discovered where he shot himself. A week after his death, a resignation letter was found in the bottom of his briefcase. In it he explained how he was just tired of all the criticism. There was absolutely nothing unusual or unexplained about Foster's suicide. We know this because Ken Starr investigated the suicide and said there was nothing out of the ordinary.[1] If there was a conspiracy, then Ken Starr was in on it, which I find hard to believe.

But that's what you're up against when you're dealing with dittoheads. The fact-free gibberish gets so ingrained in your psyche that even when you come to your senses there's still some stuff in there that you can't get out. Or that you forgot was still in there.

We Won't Win by Out-Hating Them

There are those in the liberal/progressive community who believe that all of conservatism is based in hate, that conservatives are all the same and that there's no point in trying to reason with them. That's a big mistake. A good way to dissuade our political brethren from making this mistake is to point out that Rush does the exact same thing: Rush defines liberals as this homogeneous group with crazy, hate-filled ideas as to how government should work.

But hate only gets you so far, and I'll say from experience that I don't think we should counter what the right is doing by defining conservatives as a homogeneous group with crazy, hate-filled ideas. We're not going to win a lot of converts by out-hating them. That just escalates the level of dissonance.

Much of the conservative worldview is based on ignorance. If the problem stems from ignorance, then the solution is knowledge, not hate. For example, I hated abortion because I'd never known anyone who'd had one. In my ignorance, I assumed that only selfish, hedonistic women have abortions. That was about to change in a big way, and my conservative worldview was about to receive its first cuts.

3 : AMY'S STORY

•

I'm going to call her Amy. (That isn't her name.) I met Amy in college. At the time, I was pretty vocal about my pro-life stance, saying things like, "You can kill a baby in the womb, but you can't kill a baby eagle." I borrowed that saying from my dad, who used to use this kind of example all the time. "You can kill a baby in the womb, but you can't do X," where X equals some absurd but, in his mind, widely held liberal viewpoint. He probably got it from Rush, who would say things like, "It's a felony to step on a spotted-owl egg, but it's fine to kill a human life in a woman's womb."

Amy heard me use this line, and it got us talking about abortion. I told her I was pro-life, and that I was going to take part in a Tennessee Right to Life protest at a local abortion clinic. I was pretty excited—it was going to be my first protest!

She asked me why I thought protesting was necessary. The

answer for me at the time was simple. "If we don't protest, then women will think that abortion is okay. It's important for there to be a stigma attached to abortion, otherwise everyone will have one." It was the classic conservative notion that well-to-do white women are ripping fully formed fetuses out of their bodies so they can resume their lives of alcoholism and debauchery. "The way I look at it, the woman already made a choice to have sex out of wedlock. Now it's time for her to take personal responsibility for having sex before she got married." That's the exact wording I used when I called in to a local radio talk show in Knoxville to help spread the gospel. At no point did "the child" enter into my argument. Looking at it now, I realize that for me being "pro-life" was really more about being anti-premarital sex. Which was hypocritical of me, as I had already engaged in premarital sex. (And it never even occurred to me that a married woman might have an abortion.)

Amy asked that I first listen to her story, and if afterward I still wanted to go protest, that was fine with her. Being a fearless Republican of core principles, I agreed. I thought her story would be about some slutty friend of hers who'd had an abortion. But I was mistaken. It wasn't a story about a friend; it was Amy's story.

Amy had fallen in love at the age of 15. Her boyfriend—let's call him Rod—was 18. His parents were rich, he was popular, smart, talented, and was about to attend a good college. He also knew that he was popular, smart, and talented, and he treated people that way, Amy included.

They had sex. Rod didn't wear protection. A few weeks later Amy missed her period. She bought a pregnancy test, which confirmed what she already suspected. She wanted to tell her parents, but was scared to death of how they would react because they were both very religious. When I confronted myself with the reality of her situation, I understood why. I was scared to death to come home with a D on my report card; I could only imagine how "Hey dad . . . got my girlfriend pregnant" would go over. To say nothing of "Hey dad . . . I'm pregnant."

Amy told Rod she was pregnant, and he went ballistic. "I'm not the father! And I'm not letting this screw up my life!" He said she'd been sleeping around. He then stormed off, and even though Amy never said so, I got the impression that before he left he got violent.

The next day at school, Rod was running around telling everyone what a slut Amy was. That way, when she announced that she was pregnant, Rod had an alibi. Since Rod was supremely popular, naturally everyone believed him. Needless to say, Amy was devastated. Suddenly she's a pariah, and if she tells anyone she's pregnant, her 15-year-old life will be over.

Dazed and confused, Amy told her parents what happened, and they responded by kicking her out of the house, saying that they couldn't handle the stigma that having a pregnant 15-year-old would bring on them in church. I always knew churches were important in Southern social circles, but I never realized they could be used as a reason to ostracize your daughter.

Amy then moved in with a friend, who told her she'd have to move out before she started to show or her parents would freak. At this point, Amy was at an understandable low point. Her parents have disowned her, the love of her life is spreading lies about her, and as soon as she starts to look pregnant she's going to become homeless. She's weak, vulnerable . . . and right on cue, Rod returned.

Apparently word had gotten back to Rod's parents that Amy was pregnant. And they put a bug in Rod's ear that he might be required to take a paternity test, which could destroy his happy life of privilege. So Rod went to see Amy, said he was sorry for what he did, sorry for how he'd behaved, and that he wanted her back. But he wasn't ready to start a family. He told Amy that if she had an abortion, he'd pay for it, and in a few years when he was out of college, they could get married and have kids together.

From Amy's perspective, she was about to get the best of all possible worlds. She could tell her parents that she wasn't really pregnant after all, but had just missed her period. Then they'd take her back. If people at school saw her with Rod, then the rumors of her being a slut would go away. Best of all, she'd really have Rod back, and in a few years when he finished college, they'd get to have kids for real.

Amy went to the clinic. A bunch of us right-to-lifers were there to get in a few parting "killer, sinner, whore" chants. Amy used the money Rod gave her to have the abortion. The next day, Rod dumped her.

For the pro-life crowd, blame begins and ends with the woman—her choices, her decision, her sin. But after hearing Amy's story, I realized that a lot of people share the responsibility—in her case, Rod for abandoning her, her parents for not supporting her, and even the church for fostering the kind of atmosphere in which it was easier for a family to disown a child than accept reality.

This was all very different from my Rush-inspired understanding of abortion. This wasn't a story about a selfish hedonist intent on self-destructive behavior. This was the story of a girl abandoned by everyone, including her family, and ultimately taken advantage of by someone she thought she loved. It was a story of youthful misjudgment. It was the story of an unwanted pregnancy, and it made me think that maybe we should take steps to stop *those* rather than just try to outlaw abortion. Treat the illness, not the symptom.

But thanks to Rush and his "feminazis," it would be years before I understood that you could be pro-choice *and* want fewer abortions. That thought process is anathema to the dittohead mindset, which says, "Being pro-choice means you want to kill every single unborn child." In fact, banning abortion wouldn't stop the procedure any more than banning drugs has stopped their abuse. Furthermore, abortion is medically necessary in certain cases. I don't want a mother to die because a procedure that could have saved her life is illegal. I think we can reduce the number of abortions in this country while at the same time keeping them safe and legal for those who need them. Furthermore, if a pregnant woman knew strong laws existed to force the father to provide for her and her child financially, that might also result in fewer abortions.

If abortion had been illegal back when Amy was pregnant, I wouldn't have put it past Rod to violently force her into a miscarriage. Or worse, he might have turned into a late-'80s Scott Peterson. However bad you think abortion is, it's way better than that alternative. Experience has taught me that we could accomplish more of the stated pro-life goals if we focus on reducing the number of unwanted pregnancies.

I didn't protest at the abortion clinic that day. Amy's is just one story, but it was a story so powerful to me that I was no longer able to be a member of the pro-life community after hearing it. I've heard many stories about abortion since then, and I'm still looking for that first remorseless, selfish, hedonistic "feminazi." I hate to burst the pro-life bubble, but I don't think that woman exists.

4 : LOVE THE GAY, HATE THE AGENDA

•

Despite no longer being a dittohead on abortion after hearing Amy's story, I still had much in common with the Republicans on social matters, particularly because of my hatred of homosexuals. Notice how the right uses the term "homosexuals" instead of "gay people"? The problem with the latter is that it includes the word "people," therefore humanizing the very group they're trying to denigrate.

For some, even the term "homosexual" isn't dehumanizing enough. For those people (myself included at the time) there needed to be something even more insidious to hate—and that something was the so-called "gay agenda." I have yet to see the "gay agenda" in document form. It's one of Rush's boogeyman words meant to scare you. "You don't want the gay agenda being taught to your kids, do you?"

When I was growing up, my dad always referred to homosexuals as "queers" so that I would know that there was "something wrong with them." He later decried the fact that homosexuals no longer found the term "queer" offensive, and were in fact using it themselves. "It used to MEAN something!" he would complain. The funny thing is, my dad has always acted normal around people that he knows are gay. He's the living embodiment of "hate the sin, love the sinner." He doesn't like homosexuality, and he wishes it would be done behind closed doors (so to speak), but he's not violently homophobic. Mostly, he just hates the "gay agenda," like I used to. As with most things dittoheaded, this hatred is based on ignorance, misunderstanding, and on occasion, outright lies.

Don't Ask, Don't Tell Me You Understand the Military, You Draft Dodger!

I first saw the "gay agenda" manifest itself in the form of President Clinton's initiative to allow gays in the military. Rush naturally decried Clinton's "don't ask, don't tell" policy, saying that the military "is no place for social experimentation." You can have your "froo-froos" in society as a whole, but keep them out of my military, thank you very much!

Rush's reasoning seemed rock solid to me at the time. Unit cohesion is paramount in combat operations, so something that could compromise that cohesion should not be allowed. You can't have Big Gay Al running limp-wristed across the battlefield to plant kisses on a fallen comrade. Go ahead and laugh, but I guarantee you that's the image that comes to mind for most dittoheads when you talk about gays in the military. And, even if you thought homosexuality was okay (which I most certainly did not), it seemed reasonable to think that this policy could cause an otherwise efficient combat unit to lose efficiency. Right or wrong, if soldiers are uncomfortable serving with homosexuals, then they shouldn't be forced to do so.

Since I was a know-it-all dittohead at the time, I eagerly took on all comers. I was like a kid who just learned a new karate move and wanted to get in a fight to see if it worked. I also wanted to look smart and dialed-in on the pressing issues of the day. (How I long for the days when gays in the military was the most pressing issue we faced.) However, most people I knew agreed with me. I was, after all, going to college in Knoxville, Tennessee. Not exactly a hotbed of liberal activity.

One day I started talking about the issue with a guy I'd known for about a year and a half. Normally I wouldn't expose one of my inner-circle friends to a political diatribe, but I was kind of tired of everyone agreeing with me, so I thought I'd take the debate to the next level—friends—in the hopes of impressing someone with my political insight.

I start telling him about "unit cohesion" and "liberal social experimentation." He took in everything I said, then responded. "I don't really care, because I have no intention of serving in the military, but you do know I'm gay, right?" I did not, and quickly ended the conversation.

As with abortion, this guy didn't fit the stereotype of what a "queer" should look like. His dorm room was always a mess, he didn't speak with a lisp, and he didn't seem to possess any extraordinary powers of fashion. He also never tried to hit on me, even though I'd been drunk in his room on many an occasion. What the hell? Like abortion, were my stereotypes about homosexuals wrong as well? Could they just be normal people? Could they look like you or me? (If they did, how could we stop them?)

After his "confession," my attitude toward him changed. I'd still hang out with him—as long as we were with other people. And even then, I tried not to stand too close to him, as I didn't want anyone thinking we were a couple. Maybe he picked up on this, because after the summer break we didn't hang out anymore. I don't blame him. I was in the early stages of overcoming homophobia, and I can't imagine too many people—and especially too many gay people—would want to stick around while someone figured that out.

Years later I discovered that my *roommate* at the time was also gay. He was so worried about my homophobia that I was the last one of his friends he outed himself to. I was reaping what I had sown. While I had come a long way from the guy with the "AIDS Island" idea, I still wasn't exactly topping the "World's Most Egalitarian" charts. It would take years, but eventually my attitude toward gay people would change from one of self-righteous inquisitor to equal rights advocate. When you stop being scared of *homosexuals*, you get to know them as *people*, and find out that they are just like everyone else.

Anne Lamott once said, "You know you've created God in your own image when He hates the same people you do." Not only is that true, but I've also found the opposite to be the case. Once I quit hating gay people, so did God. Funny how that works.

5 : WATCHING THEM MAKE SAUSAGE

•

By the time I graduated from college, I no longer hated gay people and was no longer part of the pro-life movement. Following the conservative spectrum, I had edged left, from a hardline theo-con to a fiscal conservative (having skipped the neo-con and oppressed-majority stages). In the mid- to late 90s, you could be socially liberal and fiscally conservative and still be a Republican (nowadays such an admission will have people charging you with being a RINO— "Republican in Name Only" or worse, "un-American"), and you could certainly still be a dittohead.

In the process of my transformation, I had become less interested in volunteering for things like protests and political campaigns, figuring I'd leave the difficult missionary work to those farther to the right while I focused my efforts on converting those in my immediate gravitational field (friends, coworkers, family, etc.). This phenomenon helps explain by and large why dittoheads are also "slacktivists." When you spend three hours a day listening to a guy explain politics, and then spend the rest of the day trying to convert your immediate circle, you feel like you've done your duty, and don't have to lend any official help to a campaign or a protest. By simple repeating what Rush says, you're doing your part. Membership in this broadcast equivalent of a country club was the only satisfaction I required in my political life.

That changed for me in 1999. By then I hated Clinton and everything he stood for (thanks in part to Rush constantly pointing out all the things Clinton did that were supposedly going to wreck the economy). I didn't want to see four years of Al Gore, and I liked the idea of Bush's son getting elected. It just felt right. Like the nation could say, "Electing Clinton was a big mistake! We're sorry, George Sr. We'll elect your son to show how wrong we are." I called it "Bush 2000: The Apology."

I was on board with Dubya early on in the campaign. When I found out that Candidate Bush was going to speak in Memphis, I decided to turn off the radio and actually do something. A few years later, a friend of mine who's a lobbyist explained to me that "watching politics unfold is like watching someone make sausage. You may really enjoy the end result, but you definitely don't want to know what goes into making it." He was right, as I was about to find out.

An old family friend was a local Republican alderman, well connected within the local party. I'd been in touch with him a few times for some professional advice (we're both in the insurance business), and one time I asked him how I could get involved with Bush-Cheney 2000. He said the best thing for me to do would be to join the Shelby County Young Republicans. That seemed odd. I was 27 at the time, and wasn't sure I qualified as a "young" anything anymore. But he insisted that the SCYR was the minor leagues for the "grown-up" Republican Party, and that if I wanted to be a big boy Republican one day, I'd have to pay my dues.

I went to my first meeting at a great little BBQ joint in East Memphis called Willingham's. The room where the meeting was being held was dark, but then so was most of the restaurant, so I didn't think much about it. There were about 15 or 20 people present, mostly women, and just about all of them in their late teens or early 20s. Some of them struck me as people I would have avoided in high school, but probably would have slept with in college.

I've joined a lot of organizations in my professional life. When you go for the first time, someone immediately comes up to you with that hugely unnatural smile, "is so excited to see you," and walks you through the initiation process. So I thought it odd when no one said a word to me. Instead, everyone was intently hunched over long restaurant tables, working on something that I couldn't make out. When they saw me, they covered up what they were doing and gave me a look that said, "Who sent you? You're not supposed to be here!" So I hung back in a corner of the room, thinking that maybe the "hospitality manager" hadn't shown up yet.

Eventually, a guy sidles up to me, and introduces himself as Chris. (I should tell you at this point that I am not using anyone's real name.) He is about a decade older than me, and I'm thinking, "I don't want to be in my late 30s and still be a Young Republican. Just how long is this dues paying period?" Chris was a guy who wouldn't have hung out with *me* in high school. He greets me with a noncommittal "hey." I introduce myself, telling him that I'm a lifelong dittohead and was hoping to do some work for the Bush campaign. He's not excited, and introduces me to a guy named Ron who then in turn introduces me to Dan, who is the hospitality manager. So, it took two people to introduce me to the guy who is supposed to introduce himself to me. In addition, Dan has the most depressing voice I've ever heard in my life—like South Park's Mr. Mackey mixed with high levels of Prozac. I avoid Dan.

Right before the meeting starts, I finally realize what everybody's been doing, what they felt they had to hide from me. They're making signs. You know, those little homemade signs with glitter and glue. On the signs they're writing slogans like "Bush Is Best" and "No More Gore." I figured that they must be making their own signs for the rally. But then I notice that when one of the girls finishes her sign, she starts working on another.

Eventually, Ron starts the meeting and Chris comes back over to stand next to me. I ask him about the girl, and why she's making a second sign. Is she going to wave them both? Or does she have a backup in case some of the glitter flies off her first sign? Chris gives me one of those "You're so cute" laughs, and explains that she's making signs to *hand out* at the Bush rally. That was a bit off-putting. Naive as it may sound, I always figured the people waving signs at rallies actually *made* them. Somehow I thought activist democracy involved at least taking the time to make your own sign. (Turns out that at the Bush-

Cheney rallies in 2004, you were forbidden to enter with a homemade sign. Those hand-painted signs you saw being waved were made by the local Young Republicans.)

Ron immediately gets everyone excited by announcing, officially, that Candidate Bush will be making a stop in Memphis the following Tuesday. (Good news for the people making the signs.) This seems strange too, as I already knew Bush was coming . . . because it was in the newspaper. Everyone goes crazy anyway (or at least as crazy as a group of teenage and 20-something Republicans can get). My mind is racing as I wonder what my assignment will be. Will I help form people into lines to get into the event? Maybe I'll be handing out some of those signs? Whatever I wind up doing, big or small, I am just happy to be part of this, and to be able to support Bush!

Ron goes on to tell us that the job of the Shelby County Young Republicans will be to take the signs we've made, find the protesters and . . . wait for the CAMERAS to show up. "Why do we care about the cameras?" I wonder to myself. Ron goes on to say that we are to insert ourselves BETWEEN the protesters and the cameras to make it look as though everyone is there to support Bush. My jaw dropped. We were going to use signs to deceive the cameras in order to deceive those watching the event on television. I realized I had just witnessed the making of sausage.

Now, maybe it was silly of me to be morally outraged that the Republican Party lies to try to make it look as though protesters are really supporters. Maybe this sort of behavior is par for the course in politics. But I can tell you that when I campaigned for Kerry in 2004, we didn't pull any of that kind of stuff. If that's why we lost, then I don't have the will to do what it takes to win. Call me crazy, but if the only way you can get elected (or reelected) is to campaign on a series of lies, there's something morally bankrupt with your party.

That did it for my participation in the Young Republicans. Except that every week for the next year or so, Dan would call my house and leave a message. "Hey Jim. It's Dan. We're real excited about our guest at the Young Republicans meeting this week. He's Doug Gnutsak, the assistant secretary to the tertiary adjunct to the mayor. It's going to be real exciting. We hope you can be there, m'kay? M'kay."

Despite my reservations about the Young Republicans, on November 7, 2000, I enthusiastically pulled the lever for George W. Bush. Then, like much of the rest of the nation, I held my breath for a few months. My wife (a lifelong Democrat) and I had had surprisingly few conversations about the election beforehand. (The one we had involved whether or not I could put a Bush-Cheney 2000 sign in our front yard. She said if I did that she'd put out a Gore-Lieberman 2000 sign. I couldn't live with one of those in my front yard, so I dropped the whole idea.)

Our heated moments came after the election, during the interminable period while we waited for the Supreme Court to decide who won. She'd voted for Gore, but didn't expect him to win. It was only after it looked like Gore had a chance that she got irritated at me for supporting Bush. However, the closeness of the race didn't bother me. Like most dittoheads, I was pretty sure we'd find out that thousands of dead people had voted for Gore in Florida, and that the race really wasn't as close as it seemed. I exhaled when the Supreme Court called off the recount. It was over. Bush had won.

Months after Bush was sworn in, the AP released its findings on the recount effort. The only way Bush would have lost the recount was if the entire state were recounted. This was ironic because that's what Bush wanted to do if a recount was to proceed. Gore just wanted to recount specific counties, which wouldn't have given him enough votes to win.

Later I would find out about the felon list, whereby thousands of African-Americans were purged from the voter rolls, not because they were felons, but because they had the same *name* as a felon.[1] This wasn't a mistake—it was cheating. And to me it was worse than finding out about dead people voting. It represented the deliberate silencing of a legal, voting minority. And I hope Republicans start catching a lot more hell for doing things like this.

But before we get to payback for the 2000 election, there's something else I've got to deal with: September 11, and how it resulted in my temporary transformation from "dittohead" to "dittiot."

6 : 9/11 CHANGED EVERYTHING

•

By 2001, Republicans controlled the House, the Senate (until "Jumping" Jim Jeffords left the reservation), the White House, and it seemed, the Supreme Court. Unemployment was low, wages were high, and we were going to get a tax cut that would in turn increase federal revenue, just like it did under Reagan. Even the "death tax" was going away. As a dittohead, there wasn't all that much to be upset about. While I still thought that Republicans held the upper hand on national defense and foreign policy, I had become more of a left-leaning Republican. I thought the big story of 2001 was going to be how Americans were sick to death of paying a buck to use another bank's ATM. These are what we today call "elegant problems."

Maybe it was because we'd finally won control of the government, but it seemed like Rush was now out of touch. He spent an awful lot of time talking about how great his new Gulf

Stream jet was, and about all the famous people he was hanging out with, such as a PGA Golf Tour buddy who had given him a set of Tour Pro clubs. Rush said that they were really hard to use, but he was going to marshal the triumphant power of personal responsibility to overcome this difficult obstacle. Talk about your elegant problems.

Then 9/11 happened, and as the cliché goes, everything changed.

9/11 was the Pearl Harbor or Kennedy assassination of my generation. Like everyone else, I remember where I was when it happened. I was in an Office Max when the clearly distressed clerk who was ringing up my paper and toner told me authoritatively that a 727 had *accidentally* crashed into the World Trade Center.

"Accidental, my ass," I immediately thought. This was terrorism, pure and simple. Didn't she remember 1993?

It was in the car on my way to work that I heard about the second plane. At that point even the news anchors realized this wasn't an accident. It was a terrorist attack. Then I heard about the Pentagon. Then another crash in Pennsylvania. This wasn't just terrorism anymore—it was war. It was also the beginning of the end of my flirtation with liberalism. I still viewed Republicans as the final arbiter on military issues, and suddenly national defense had become our most important policy issue.

However, my first question was "where's Bush?" Rudy Giuliani was masterful, saying we'd get over this, and that those responsible would be brought to justice. While I was pleased to hear this, I'd much rather be hearing it from the commander-in-chief.

The initial reports were sketchy, but it was pretty clear that Bush was in hiding. When he made a disorganized statement from an "undisclosed location," I was not too happy. A real leader would have gone back to D.C. immediately. What was wrong with this guy? Eventually he made it back to the White House, and news reports came out saying he boldly told his advisors they could go to hell if they thought it was unsafe for him to return. That helped to make amends.

God Bless . . . Afghanistan?

In the months immediately following the attacks, there was an amazing level of bipartisanship in the government. When congressmen began singing "God Bless America" on the steps of the Capitol, I had tears in my eyes. While I didn't believe for a moment that it was spontaneous, in that place and time I didn't care. It was a beautiful moment.

Then the war in Afghanistan came . . . and went. That was easy. It felt like we sent in 30 guys for a weekend of backpacking, and while we were there we overthrew the Taliban. There was no video feed from inbound ordinance. No footage of hundreds of tanks rolling across the open desert. We just got patient updates from the military. It was like a war fought in another time. One could imagine throngs of reporters flying out of the military press conferences to simultaneously hit the pay phones to call in their story. Or thousands of U.S. paratroopers making static jumps from hundreds of WWII-era C-47s. I half expected updates from the front lines to be read in telegraph format. "To Commander, Atlantic Forces. STOP. Enemy spotted at Alpha, Bravo, Zulu Seven-two-niner. STOP. Will engage after a light lunch. STOP." Even CBS went with the retro feel. While all the other news networks were using high-resolution video maps of the region, Dan Rather and company gathered around an actual, physical plaster cast of Afghanistan. It looked more like an eighth-grade science project than a newsworthy prop. I kept expecting to see baking soda lava erupt from Mt. Sikeram.

Where Is Osama?

Like anyone else, I thought that the key point of the war with Afghanistan was to capture Osama bin Laden. And, like everyone else, I wanted him captured, but unlike most people, I didn't want to see him killed. Not out of any mixed emotions I may have had about the death penalty. (I was very much for it at the time.) I wanted Osama alive because I wanted him broken. Dead, he was a martyr. Alive and in jail, he was a reminder—a reminder that if you mess with us, you pay a price. For bin Laden, that price was going to be a lifetime of prison sex, and I couldn't think of a punishment more befitting a militant Muslim. Little did I know that my personal revenge fantasy would be played out at Abu Ghraib, and it would apply not to Osama, but to random detainees who were in the wrong place at the wrong time.

The dénouement of the Afghan war came at Tora Bora (or as confused voters called it after the Bush-Kerry debates, "Bora Bora"). Like a good '50s gangster movie, we had Osama surrounded. All that was left was for him to come out with his hands up. Unfortunately this wasn't a good '50s gangster movie; it was a bad '60s Bond movie, and Osama got in his escape pod and flew away vowing revenge. Mullah Omar (does anyone even remember him?) flew the coop as well. Still, while they may have gotten away this time, I knew we'd get them in the sequel. And I certainly knew that none of this was Bush's fault. This is what bad guys do—they get away.

The Blame Game

As the Afghan war ended, so too ended the spirit of bipartisanship. Both sides began pointing fingers at who was really responsible for 9/11. Republicans, like they do with everything—I mean, *everything*—blamed Clinton. Democrats pointed out that Bush was in charge when it happened, so it was his fault.

For my part, I blamed neither. Bush had only been in office nine months. Sure he spent a lot of that time on vacation, but they were *working* vacations. And it's not like he'd been getting memos saying "Bin Laden Determined to Attack within the U.S." How was he supposed to know? I didn't blame Clinton either because, frankly, the political will didn't exist pre-9/11 to do what needed to be done against bin Laden. If you're going to be intellectually honest, when you say 9/11 changed everything, you have to accept that things were different *before* as well as *after*.

But Rush, as usual, had an interesting approach. In an attempt to remain cloaked in a spirit of bipartisanship, he would act outraged while at the same time blaming the other side. "I can't believe the Democrats are trying to politicize 9/11 when it's so clearly Clinton's fault." Then came the allegations that Clinton was offered Osama on a "silver platter" but didn't do anything. Rush even had audio of Clinton bemoaning the fact that he didn't have anything to charge Osama with, and how he had begged the Saudis to take him into custody.

At the time, I assumed this was an accurate representation of what had happened, but I still didn't hate Clinton for it. Maybe I was just tired of hating Clinton. After eight years, you just get tired of feeling angry all the time. But more to the point, I was trying to be honest about conditions pre-9/11. Had Clinton gone after bin Laden, the dittohead nation would've called it another "Monica's War," just like it did when he kicked Milosevic out of Kosovo.

Rush's all-out assault on Clinton continued, and expanded. Clinton was responsible for 9/11. This was the Clinton recession. Clinton was Deep Throat. Clinton killed the Lindberg baby! While this was "red meat" for the dittohead nation, I thought it was unnecessary and self-destructive. Why focus on the past when there was so much more important going on?

That answer became clear as we prepared for war with Iraq.

7: IRAQ: MY PERSONAL ROAD TO DAMASCUS

•

I've known several self-described "lapsed Catholics" in my life, and there's one thing they've all had in common—while they will admit they don't go to church anymore and don't really believe in much of the Church's doctrine, they will defend the Catholic faith like a grizzly protecting its cubs if you say anything bad about it. That's how I was with the Republican Party by 2002—I'd seen the party's warts, but I'd be damned if I was going to sit idly by while Democrats pointed those warts out.

"You liberals just don't get it!" I thought. "Everyone *knows* Saddam has huge stockpiles of WMDs, a continuing and thriving nuclear weapons program, and clear collaborative ties to Al Qaeda. There's even substantial evidence that the 9/11 hijackers trained exclusively in Iraq."

How did I know all this? Rush told me, of course. During the buildup to the Iraq war, Rush was my sole source for news and commentary. Needless to say, this was a dangerous thing. Rush operates in one of two ways. In his less damaging mode, he will take something said by a way-left-fringe liberal and say that that point represents the "mainstream" of Democratic thought. More insidiously, though, he will take an otherwise innocuous comment made by a Democrat and then tell you what it "really" means. Needless to say, Rush usually goes flying down a slippery slope like it's a Slip-N-Slide covered with Crisco. In the months leading up to 9/11, I had started taking Rush's assertions with a grain of salt. But after 9/11, I took them as seriously as an addict takes prescription painkillers.

You're on the cusp of dittiotism when you stop finding things out for yourself and let Rush tell you what to think. However, you've still got one step left—despite your belief in all things Rush, you still want confirmation of his "facts." So, at Rush's suggestion, you turn to Fox News. That's when the circle is finally closed, and you're officially a dittiot.

On the surface, it doesn't necessarily seem like a problem to get your news from people who agree with you politically. Your average dittohead will argue that liberals get their news from the liberal media, so why is it bad for them to get their news from the conservative media? Unfortunately, the truth is (and this is going to get a lot of pushback from your dittohead friends), there's no such thing as the liberal media. This is a hard concept for dittoheads to grasp. (It took me 13 years to realize it.) But eventually you have to grow up and realize that there's no such thing as the Tooth Fairy, Santa Claus, or the Liberal Media.

Dittoheads believe that the bias of the liberal media is not necessarily overt. It can be a tone, or a gesture, or the type of story that's selected to air. A mainstream reporter will never say, "This is another victory for the president . . . and another staggering defeat for mankind."

On the other hand, the conservative media will come right out and say, "Yeah, we're conservative. Don't like it? Screw you!" Let me throw a couple of examples at you, and see if you can find a place where a mainstream "liberal" media anchor or reporter would say something similar:

"I think that these kinds of problems and accusations [about prisoner abuse at Guantánamo] and so forth grow out of a community that stretches from the American left through much of Europe to enemies across the world from which terrorism springs, who want the world to believe that America is what's wrong with the world, or is in danger always of being what's wrong with the world, and if this administration starts yielding to those critics, it will be a very perilous path." (**Brit Hume, June 12, 2005, on** *Fox News Sunday*)

"[The] BBC almost operates as a foreign registered agent of Hezbollah and some of the other Jihadist groups." (**Fox News terrorism expert Steve Emerson, July 7, 2005, on** *The O'Reilly Factor*)

" . . . the International Olympic Committee missed a golden opportunity today. If they had picked France, if they had picked France instead of London, to hold the Olympics, it would have been the one time we could look forward to where we didn't worry about terrorism. They'd blow up Paris, and who cares?" (**Fox News host John Gibson, July 6, 2005, on** *The Radio Factor with Bill O'Reilly*)

"Some pundits have said they thought [Al Gore] went off his meds." (**Linda Vester, May 27, 2004, on Fox News's** *DaySide with Linda Vester*)

There's the difference in a nutshell—the "liberal media" reports the news, but Fox News reports their *opinions* on the news. Deep down, even as a dittohead, you know the difference, but at the tipping point of dittiotism you equate the two. Fox is "Fair and Balanced" not because they actually are, but because they provide balance to the mainstream liberal media. They provide news from the "conservative perspective," making it sound as though news lacks any objective element at all. It's like saying the headline "London subways bombed" is the same as the headline "Paris inexplicably not bombed like London subways."

So, as a dittiot, in order to attain "fairness and balance" to the liberal media, you believe everything that is reported by Rush Limbaugh and Fox News. And the real kicker is that you *know* that if Rush or Fox actually did get something wrong, the mainstream liberal media would be all over it. This provides dittiots with an insurance policy against being lied to by the conservative media. Never mind the fact that dittiots never actually *watch* the mainstream liberal media.

On top of all that, the dittiot mind has a remarkable ability to compartmentalize. Things that support the dittiot worldview go in the inbox; things that contradict it go in the circular file. "Good facts" go over here, "true facts" over there. It's not entirely unlike a filter you might set up for your email. Things marked "Rush," "Fox," "Hannity," and "Coulter" are allowed. Things marked CBS, NBC, ABC, CNN, *Time*, *Newsweek*, *New York Times*, *Washington Post*, Reuters, Associated Press, *Entertainment Weekly*, *Vanity Fair*, etc. go directly into the recycle bin.

So, by 2002, I found myself ensconced inside the closed circle of the right-wing media. It's like a womb, safe and quiet, with no one disagreeing with you, and the only thing that gets in is what comes through the right-wing media's carefully monitored umbilical cord. The unfortunate thing about life in the womb is that at some point you're born. Then you face the real world, and a lot of what happens is not like life in the womb. However, unlike a biological birth, as a dittiot you have the option of crawling back into the womb. You tell yourself things like "yeah, maybe that point is wrong, but Rush still gets the big picture," or "well, maybe that story was false, but it was based on the best information he had at the time. I'm sure he corrected it and I just didn't hear it." Crawl back in the womb, reattach the umbilical cord, quit thinking for yourself.

Mission Accomplished?

The first time I ever listened to Sean Hannity was during Gulf War II, where the coverage on Sean's show was all Iraq, all the time. He'd speak to generals, soldiers, and reporters on the ground, and every day, he'd give front-line updates that completely contradicted what I was hearing on the mainstream media. Take for example, the Jessica Lynch story.

One of our supply convoys was ambushed, and members of the 507th Maintenance Company were either killed or taken prisoner. One of the prisoners, Jessica Lynch, put up such a fight that she single-handedly killed dozens of Iraqis. Out of ammo, her legs and back broken, Jessica still managed to kill two more Iraqis with a knife before passing out. Later, in a daring pre-dawn raid, a joint Army Ranger and U.S. Navy SEAL team rescued Jessica, thanks to intelligence provided by an Iraqi lawyer who risked his life to save Jessica's.

The bottom line to this story was that we were winning. *One of our soldiers was more than a match for the entire Iraqi army.* Furthermore, the Iraqi people understood that we were fighting for them, and they were helping us achieve victory. Sean was right, and the mainstream media was wrong. The Jessica Lynch story confirmed everything I thought about the validity of the right-wing media.

In addition to providing positive news, the Lynch story served to underscore what I already believed—that the people who opposed the war hated Bush. At this point I became an official right-wing media junkie. I decided to completely tune out all non-Fox media for the duration of "active combat operations" in Iraq.

For me, the first sign that things might not be as they appeared on Fox News came when the Iraqis could only bring down that statue of Saddam with massive amounts of American help. I was watching it live on Fox, thinking, "Hurry up and get this damn thing done so we can all get on with our lives!" I'm still saying that today, but for different reasons.

Finally, mercifully, the statue came down, and 30 or 40 Iraqis took to the streets to celebrate by riding Saddam's head barefoot and clapping with their shoes. The next day Sean was practically in tears describing the beautiful scene in which thousands of Iraqis took to the streets to celebrate the statue coming down. I was thinking, "Thousands?"

There's this apocryphal story about Carmen Electra catching Dennis Rodman in bed with another woman while they were still married. Carmen asks Dennis how he could do this to her. Dennis replies, "Do what?" "How could you be sleeping with another woman?" Carmen replies. "What woman?" Dennis asks. "That woman right there in our bed." "What are you talking about? There ain't no woman here." "But I'm looking right at her!" Carmen shouts. "Come on, baby, who you gonna believe? Me or your eyes?"

Being a dittiot is like that. At some point the truth is right there in front of you, jumping up and down, naked as a jaybird, and Sean or Rush will say, "What truth? The truth is that people who oppose the president are traitors!" Who you gonna believe, baby? Me or your eyes?

Predictably, I let my concerns about the fictional "thousands" of freedom-loving Iraqis go, which seemed like a good decision when a few months later my man, President George W. Bush, donned the flight suit and raised the "Mission Accomplished" banner to the roof of the U.S.S. *Abraham Lincoln*. Major combat operations were over. We'd won!

Now that major combat operations were over, things in Iraq . . . got worse! At first, a few G.I.s were killed while standing in line at a store or after being abducted by armed insurgents. That was bad, but surely these were just isolated incidents being sensationalized by the liberal media to make President Bush look bad.

Then the casualties started to mount. "Well, what did you expect?" the dittiot part of my brain told me. "There are a lot of people whose livelihood depended on Saddam's being in power. They weren't just going to roll over and die because they lost the war." And so I was again able to put all doubt behind me.

However, when the number of fatalities *after* "Mission Accomplished" exceeded the number *before* it, I started to worry. This didn't seem to be going particularly well. The liberal media did its part to push me back, though, by starting early and unfounded comparisons to Vietnam. Rush's response was to say that, at the current rate of U.S. fatalities, we'd have to be in Iraq for over 100 years to reach the same level of fatalities in Vietnam. Though it seemed an especially cruel calculus, it did accomplish the goal of allaying my fears.

Fox News further calmed my frayed nerves when Brit Hume made the claim that fatalities in Iraq at the time (277 after 160 days) were far lower than the average annual number of murders in California (2300).[1] California and Iraq are roughly the same size geographically, so clearly it's safer to be a soldier in Iraq than a citizen in California, right? Except that California has a population of about 38 million, and there were only 150,000 U.S. soldiers in Iraq at the time. I never thought about it like that, though. Why bother? If Brit were wrong to say it, the liberal media would've been all over him. And if that had happened, Rush would've told me that the liberal media was just going after a conservative for speaking the truth. See how tightly closed this circle is?

But the fatalities kept coming, and each day it looked more and more like the administration had absolutely no idea how to handle what was going on. The wheels really came off for me in Fallujah. In April 2004, U.S. Marines entered the city of Fallujah, which at the time was a hotbed of insurgent activity. If you remember, the objective was to capture or kill the radical cleric Moqtada Al-Sadr. Three days in, however, Bush changed his mind and told the marines to get out. Fallujah would police itself. Instead of policing itself, Fallujah became a safe harbor for the insurgency. Untold hundreds, if not thousands, would die from car bombs and improvised explosive devices made in this "self-policing" city. And we never captured Moqtada Al-Sadr.

At that point I had to ask the question, "What exactly are we dying for over there?" What exactly does it do for morale if you can kill American soldiers and never be held accountable? How am I supposed to believe that we're taking this war seriously when killers are allowed to go free? Isn't this negotiating with the terrorists?

This didn't fit the "black & white" rules of being a dittiot. With a painful slowness, and at a terrible cost, the veil of dittiotism was being slowly lifted from my eyes. The reality of Iraq around the end of 2003 coupled with the liberal social beliefs that I had developed over the past decade was moving me away from the Republican Party. From there it would take just one last straw to make me a Democrat.

8 : FROM HANNITY TO HUMANITY

•

As things got worse in Iraq, Sean Hannity needed a new bad guy. He obviously couldn't make the Iraqi insurgency the enemy—that would make it sound legitimate and not in its "last throes." Since Osama had gotten away, he obviously didn't want to focus on Al Qaeda. So who did he choose to vilify? Democrats. This seemed like a waste of energy to me. Republicans controlled everything, so why waste a second worrying about the minority party? And Sean wouldn't just waste a second, he'd waste three hours a day, every day. And that's when I realized Sean's biggest weakness—he just can't stop being Sean!

Take, for example, the following statements:[1]

HANNITY: "You could explain something about your magazine [*The Nation*]. Liza Featherstone writing about the hate America march, the [anti-war] march that took place over the weekend . . . " (*Hannity and Colmes,* 1/22/03)

HANNITY: (to attorney Stanley Cohen) "Is it that you hate this president or that you hate America?" (*Hannity and Colmes,* 4/30/03)

HANNITY: "Governor, why wouldn't anyone want to say the Pledge of Allegiance, unless they detested their own country or were ignorant of its greatness?" (*Hannity and Colmes,* 6/12/03)

HANNITY: "I never questioned anyone's patriotism." (*The Sean Hannity Radio Program,* 9/18/03)

Describing someone who questioned the president's policies as "giving aid and comfort to the enemy" was troubling to me. Using the dictionary's definition of treason to describe those who disagree with you sent up a red flag in my mind. Especially when I was one of the people questioning the policies.

The more I watched Sean, the more he started to bother me. He was just so over the top, and he never really engaged in any significant discourse. Plus, he was so full of hate. And after years of hating Democrats, hating Clinton, I'd had enough with hating. I wanted to be happy. And the only way for me to be happy was to stop watching Sean Hannity.

The Light at the End of the Dittiot Tunnel

One night I was on the phone with a friend of mine when I started groaning. My friend asked what was up. "Sean Hannity is on. Hang on, I'll be right back." I got up and turned off the radio. Returning to the phone, we started talking about Sean. My friend had never actually heard him, but he knew of him from Al Franken's book *Lies and the Lying Liars Who Tell Them*. He said the description of Hannity's show in the book was pretty funny, but he didn't know how accurate it was until he spoke to me. He offered to let me borrow his copy of the audio book the next time I saw him.

Even though I knew he had written *Rush Limbaugh Is a Big Fat Idiot*, I had liked Al Franken since I was a kid. Growing up in the 1970s, my family had had an early form of the VCR (the one with the giant tape-recorder buttons and the two huge dials on the front for changing the channel). My father used to tape *Saturday Night Live*, and one of our favorite bits was "The Franken and Davis Show." Among our favorite skits from it was a send-up of political attack ads between two fictional politicians, Winfield Adcock (Tom Davis) and Pete Tagliani (Al Franken). The bit plays out as a series of commercials. In Adcock's first commercial, he asks to be reelected. Then, in Tagliani's commercial, he says why *he* should be elected. In the next round of ads they exchange modest attacks; it escalates when Tagliani accuses Adcock of filing a bogus tax return. Adcock then accuses Tagliani of being a homosexual, claiming that Pete once tried to hit on his cousin in a men's room. (As proof, he shows a photo of Tagliani at a urinal talking to the guy next to him.) Tagliani counters that Adcock is an abusive alcoholic, and that his last name isn't even Adcock. Finally, a clearly drunk Adcock is about to deliver his coup de grace (a manila folder labeled "Solid Evidence," which he introduces by saying, "I have here . . . Solid Evidence . . . "), when Pete Tagliani runs onto the set of the ad and shoots him.

Putting the audiotape of Al's book on in my car, I vowed that I would only listen to the part about Sean Hannity. To my surprise, I literally had to stop the car, I was laughing so hard. According to Al, Sean Hannity in person is just like Sean Hannity on TV or the radio—hot-headed, arrogant, and kind of thick.

I decided to listen further, to the chapter on Ann Coulter. Even though I didn't know all that much about her, what I knew I didn't like. I'd seen her on Hannity's TV show, and when the two of them got together, it was like a couple of cackling old ladies, going back and forth with their "Wow! Can you believe this? What are these liberals doing to our country?" shtick. Aside from being Young Republican whacking material, Ann Coulter served no purpose, as far as I was concerned.

Having been entertained by those two chapters, I decided to listen to the entire book. Whatever criticisms Al had of Rush, I figured I could handle them. Besides, my dad had set the example that it's okay to laugh at satires of people you like. On top of that, I was going to fact-check what Al said, and I was going to skewer him with the shimmering sword of truth if he said anything out of line. I didn't want to go from being a "dittiot" for Rush to a "dittiot" for Al.

As I listened to Al criticizing the Bush administration, I realized "hey, he went through the same things I did." Al's reactions to the wars in Afghanistan and Iraq closely paralleled my own. We supported both operations from the start, but eventually got bad feelings as they dragged on. I sort of felt like we left Afghanistan unfinished, and didn't have enough troops in Iraq. I didn't know the half of it. Al bird-dogged stories from *Time* magazine and elsewhere that I never would have read during my hard-line dittiot days. Not wanting to take his word for it, I read over his source material, and found his analysis to be dead on. It wasn't his "this is a lie" and "that's bad journalism" stuff about Limbaugh and Coulter that moved me. It was the "big ticket" items—like Bush's attempting to block the 9/11 Commission, and then later blaming Democrats for its slow progress. Or how the Bush campaign used "push polling" to insinuate that John McCain had an illegitimate black daughter during the 2000 primaries in South Carolina. Or the way the Republicans tried to make decorated Vietnam veteran Max Cleland look like a drunk and a coward during his Senate race. Or, worst of all, how a perpetually vacationing Bush and a perpetually short-of-time Cheney missed five separate opportunities to prevent 9/11, despite analysts' screaming that Osama bin Laden should be their No. 1 priority. Unlike right-wing journalism, most of what Al was talking about wasn't conjecture and hearsay. It was actually easy to verify from the public record.

What I couldn't find in the public record . . . well, at some point you do have to apply the principle of Occam's Razor to the debate. As principles go, it's one of my favorites—the simplest answer is usually the correct one. I would apply this newfound fearlessness to the last remaining vestige of my dittohead life—fiscal conservatism.

9 : THE DEATH OF FISCAL CONSERVATISM

•

Social conservatism is driven by emotion, but fiscal conservatism is driven by facts. And the facts prove that the market prefers a Republican administration. Not only that, but Reagan proved that tax cuts increase federal revenue, and that deficits don't matter. How did I come to this conclusion? I read *The Way Things Ought to Be* by Rush Limbaugh. And, as usual, there had been no reason for me to verify what Rush wrote by using the liberal media.

I should take some time to define what it means (or rather what it *used* to mean) to be a fiscal conservative. First and foremost, fiscal conservatives believe that government should be small, and thus should spend less money. In addition to advocating the curbing of federal spending, fiscal conservatives also believe that tax cuts stimulate the economy and therefore increase federal revenue.

The first half of that statement is hard to prove or disprove, but generally seems to make sense (at least to me.) But the second part, about tax cuts increasing federal revenue . . . that one is filled with holes the size of a Volkswagen, even though it is still to this day trumpeted by conservative organizations such as the Heritage Foundation. Here's a direct quote from their website:

"It's simple: lower tax rates = more robust economy = more federal revenue." [1]

You'd have to be some kind of idiot to disagree with that, right? (I certainly didn't.) My worldview was challenged, however, when I saw Representative Harold Ford Jr. on *Hannity and Colmes* one night. Hannity dutifully quoted from the Heritage gospel, telling Ford that tax cuts have always resulted in more money for the federal government. Congressman Ford replied, "Your viewers may want to check that out. I think they'll find that federal revenues have been in a decline for the last few years." Sean wilted like a Memphis azalea in July, hastily ending the conversation with a "well, let's just agree to disagree."

I was annoyed. Why did Sean let that one go? Everyone knows tax cuts mean more money for the government. With the confidence of a dittiot, I set out to defend that statement. That was when I came head to head with the major problem with dittiot worldview—reality often refuses to conform to your worldview.

I did a quick web search for "federal revenue" and found a link to the Congressional Budget Office. Surely I would find the proof there that I needed to refute Ford's assertion. Since Congress was controlled by the Republicans, I would be able to get the straight scoop from the CBO without having to go through the liberal media "filter." On the CBO site, I checked out federal revenue from 1999 to 2003 (in billions): [2]

1999	2000	2001	2002	2003
$1,827.5	$2,025.2	$1,991.2	$1,853.2	$1,782.3

It was true that federal revenue had declined for three straight years. This could have been trouble for my worldview, but fortunately, my years of dittohead training kicked in. A cartoonish caricature of Rush appeared to me in a thought bubble and said, "Don't you think this fact has something to do with 9/11?"

Thought-bubble Rush was right! Sure, the economy has been shrinking since 2000. After all, the stock market's been struggling these last few years. I bet our nation's Gross Domestic Product has been in a decline as well. And I'm sure the decline would be even more severe if Bush hadn't cut taxes from the near criminal level of the Clinton administration.

Another web search led me to the Department of Commerce. It's another Republican-controlled site, so once again I knew I'd be getting the truth, the whole truth, and nothing but the truth. The GDP numbers (again, in billions):[3]

1999	2000	2001	2002	2003
$9,268.4	$9,187.0	$10,128.0	$10,469.6	$10,971.2

It didn't work! The economy grew every year, even in 2001. But if the economy grew, why did federal revenue go down?

The truth is, the underlying theory behind "supply-side economics" was disproved during the Clinton administration. Think about it—if lower taxes equal higher federal revenue, doesn't it necessarily follow that higher taxes equal lower federal revenue? Yet, despite what Republicans called "the biggest tax increase in history" under Clinton, the economy grew at an average annual rate of 3.7 percent during his presidency, and federal revenue grew by $870 billion. As I write this, during the Bush presidency the economy has grown at an average annual rate of 2.52 percent, yet federal revenue *is down* by $145 billion. This clearly shows that you can't cut your way out of debt. This seems obvious to me now, but to a dittohead it's like saying there's no Santa Claus. They really do believe that you can cut your income so much that you will get a raise.

Then How Do You Explain Reagan?

One of my greatest skills as a dittohead was my ability to accept the one fact that made my point, and ignore the hundred other facts that contradicted it. The above analysis of tax cuts and federal revenue was no exception. To truly understand how the supply-side myth was propagated, you have to understand that to a dittohead, fiscal conservatism begins and ends with Ronald Reagan. He was Noah, Moses, Daniel, Christ, and Paul all rolled into one.

I still have a warm spot for Reagan. Part of me thinks it's because he was president when I grew up, and that we often have a fondness for the first authority figures we're exposed to. Reagan was also charming, witty, and intelligent (three characteristics I've found to be completely lacking in W). Reagan was also all the evidence a dittohead required as proof for supply-side economics. A common refrain from Rush's show was, "Of course tax cuts increase federal revenue. Reagan proved it."

But the reality is that Reagan's tax cut proved nothing of the sort. Conservatives argue that Reagan cut the top marginal tax rate from 75 percent to 28 percent, clearly indicating that high-income earners saw their taxes go down a whopping 47 percent. In turn, these wealthiest individuals reinvested their tax savings in their businesses by hiring more people in order to expand. On paper it sounds like a decent theory. But the IRS has a chart on their website that tells a different story—the story of the Effective Tax Rate.

Nobody talks about the effective tax rate, and I don't understand why. There's two ways to look at tax rates—the marginal rate and the effective rate. The marginal rate is what you paid on the last dollar of income you earned. The effective rate is the rate you actually paid on all of your income. If you take the total amount of taxes you paid, then divide it by the total amount of money you earned, the result is your effective tax rate.

For example, say in 2004 you and your spouse had a combined earned income of $100,000. You would have paid a 10 percent tax on the first $14,300 you earned, 15 percent on the next $43,800, and 25 percent on the rest. According to the marginal rate, you were in the 25 percent tax bracket. But that doesn't mean you paid 25 percent of your income in federal taxes. It means that for every dollar you earned *over* $100,000, you paid 25 cents in taxes. But let's break down your effective tax rate:

Earned Income	Tax Rate	Taxes Paid
$14,3000	10%	$1,430
$43,800	15%	$6,570
$41,900	25%	$10,475
$100,000		$18,475
Total Income		$100,000
Total Taxes Paid		$18,475
Effective Tax Rate		18.48%
Top Marginal Rate		25%

Even though you're in the 25 percent tax bracket, you really only paid 18.5 percent in taxes. And that's assuming you didn't claim any exemptions (even for yourself), or deductions (even the standard deduction). In reality, you probably paid less than the 18.5 percent rate because of these rules.

What caused the Reagan recovery wasn't his tax cut—it was his tax reform. William Simon, who was treasury secretary under Nixon, once said that the tax code should be simplified so it looks like "someone designed it on purpose." He was right. The old tax code was out of control. Prior to Reagan's tax reform, everything was deductible—lunch, dinner, credit card interest, depreciation. You could even deduct losses in excess of what you invested. For example, you could have invested $1,000 in a real estate investment trust (REIT) and deducted $100,000 in losses from your income taxes. Reagan said forget it—you can only deduct interest on your home and reasonable charitable contributions. And you can't write off more than you invested.

So, while the top marginal rate dropped a lot, nobody was paying 75 percent of their income in taxes in the first place. They were using a whole network of deductions to lower their effective rates to the low 20 percent range. Reagan put a stop to the deductions while simplifying the tax code and keeping the effective rate about the same.

Want proof? Of course you do. Take a look at this information from the Congressional Budget Office website showing the effective tax rates for all taxpayers, followed by a look at the effective tax rates for all individuals from 1979 to 1987:[4]

	1979	1980	1981	1982	1983	1984	1985	1986	1987
All	22.2	22.2	22.4	20.7	20.4	21.0	20.9	20.9	21.6
Individual	11.0	11.7	12.0	11.0	10.2	10.2	10.2	10.4	10.3

What this shows is that, from peak to trough, individuals saw their effective tax rate go down by 1.8 percent. That's pretty far removed from the whopping 47 percent cut in the marginal rate. It seems pretty ridiculous to assume that a 1.8 percent reduction in the rate that people actually *paid* in taxes resulted in the economic renaissance of the 1980s.

Without all those deductions that Reagan eliminated, an entire cottage industry that existed solely for the purposes of creating losses (namely REITs and limited partnerships) became worthless. That had the intended consequence of shifting a good-size portion of our economy away from loss-generating activities toward the more natural activity of making money. That's why the economy took off during the Reagan years. There wasn't a valid economic reason for loss-generating business entities to continue, so the free market got rid of them. Simple, brilliant and effective.

W Is No Reagan

Bush's problem (there are a lot of those) is that he thought Reagan's plan was successful simply because it cut taxes. It didn't. It just got rid of about a jillion loopholes while remaining revenue-neutral. In absolute terms, federal revenue increased every year Reagan was in office except for 1983, where they declined slightly. It was more or less at this point that Reagan admitted his mistake and said we needed another tax bracket. That's another big difference between Reagan and Bush—Reagan could admit when he was wrong.

One defense used by dittoheads is that Bush's economic plan hasn't had enough time to take effect. How long does it need to work? It didn't take Reagan's tax cuts any time to kick in. Here's what happened to federal revenue during Reagan's first four years in office:[5]

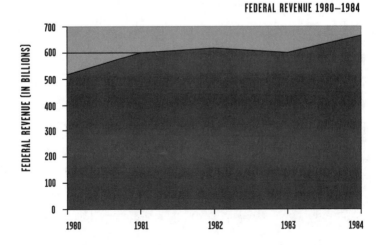

FEDERAL REVENUE 1980–1984

Either Reagan's plan worked from day one or dittoheads find themselves in the uncomfortable position of calling the period from 1980-1982 "The Carter Recovery."

Let's assume that Reagan's plan did work from day one and compare that to Bush's first four years in office:[6]

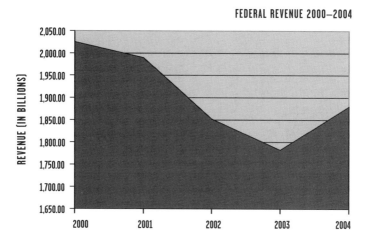

FEDERAL REVENUE 2000–2004

Reality refuses to conform to Republican doctrine! Without any facts to stand on, my dittohead mind raced to figure out how the numbers might still work out. Maybe without those tax cuts, the GDP wouldn't have grown by $2 trillion. In fact, it probably would have shrunk for three straight years, and revenue would've declined even more without Bush's tax cuts.

Unfortunately, historically, that doesn't hold a lot of water. Over the last 50 years, we've never had three consecutive years of negative GDP growth, and we've only had consecutive negative years once.[7] From 1974-75 the economy shrank by 0.5 percent and 0.2 percent respectively. As bad as that two-year number is, it's still an improvement over the worst single year in the last 50 years, 1982, when GDP declined by 1.9 percent (during the "Reagan Recession"). While negative economic activity of any kind is generally unfavorable, these numbers are still a far cry from the Great Depression, when the GDP declined by 8.6 percent, 6.4 percent, and 13 percent over a three-year period (1930-1932).

However, it's inappropriate to use the Great Depression as a model for what could have happened to our economy, because the dittohead mind will say, "That is what would've happened were it not for the tax cuts!" But the Great Depression occurred not because of an oppressive tax code, but due to a lack of regulatory restraints on our market system. Back then you could buy stocks by putting 10 percent or less down, meaning you could lose $1,000 on a $100 investment. It hasn't happened since because we have a properly regulated free market.

But that didn't stop my dittohead mind from juggling the numbers. "So what if the economy *did* decline by 0.5 percent and then by another full percent. And just for the hell of it, let's throw in another 1.5 percent in 2004 for good measure." Keep in mind that this kind of decline has never happened in the modern age of this nation, but let's pretend that without the 1-2 percent cut in the effective tax rate we would have had an economic apocalypse.

Besides the fact that Bush would have been thrown out on his ear, at that point our nation's GDP would have gone from $9,817 billion to $9,525 billion. That's still a higher level of economic activity than we had in 1999 ($9,268.4 billion); therefore one might assume that tax revenue collected would have been a little higher than revenue collected that year ($1,827.5 billion).

Let's review. With an additional $2 trillion in economic activity and tax cuts, the federal government was able to collect $1.88 billion. But if we assume no tax cuts and an unprecedented economic *contraction,* we'd have economic activity still above the level of economic activity in 1999, which would generate, say $1.88 billion in revenue.

This wasn't working. It's like a Rubik's Cube where I could only get one side to be the same color. Every time I tried to get another side, I messed up the side I'd already finished. But there was one way to get all the sides the same color—by admitting that supply-side economics don't work. That tax cuts may stimulate the economy, but they sure don't increase federal revenue in a vacuum. Reality had cremated one of the last remaining cornerstones of my Heritage Foundation–based fiscal conservatism.

The last bastion of being a traditional fiscal conservative involved balancing the budget by cutting federal spending. How's that going, you may ask? Under Bush, terribly, and even dittoheads point to this and cry foul. However, not surprisingly, most dittoheads blame the Democrats for the problem. They believe that many Republican politicians desperately want to be loved by the liberal media, so they wind up giving the Democrats everything they want in legislation like welfare, Medicare, and Social Security. That's why they believe the budget deficit is so high, because Republicans keep caving in to Democrats so they can win the approval of the liberal media.

This level of cognitive dissonance is incredible when viewed from the outside. But from the inside, it was impossible for me to see anything else! Or it would have been were it not for that appearance by a lone Democrat on *Hannity and Colmes*. A Democrat who spoke not to Sean, but directly to the viewer. I was able to meet Congressman Ford in person several months later and thanked him for being on the show. He said that if Democrats didn't go on those right-wing shows, then they'd just be talking to themselves.

By the time Congressman Ford made his appearance, many of my dittohead convictions were lying around as dead husks making a pile of tinder. Ford provided the flint. There was only one thing I still needed to light the funeral pyre of my dittiot existence: a spark . . .

10 : THE LAST STRAW

•

By 2004, I had absolutely nothing in common with the Republican Party. Every plank in the party platform had been blown away for me by the harsh hurricane of reality. But I was unwilling to "join" the Democratic Party yet. I considered myself politically independent and was sure I could remain socially liberal, but still vote Republican. After all, it's not like the Republicans were going to start trying to legislate morality!

Then it happened. On February 25, 2004, Bush announced his support for the Federal Marriage Amendment. As much as 9/11 represented a declaration of war against terrorism, February 25, 2004, represented the start of the Republican war "on things we think are immoral." It was the last straw for me. I knew I could never vote for a Republican again. At the time, my wife and I were on a ski trip in Vail, Colorado. Becky recognized the look on my face. The last vestiges of respect disappearing for someone you once voted for. "That's it, isn't it? You're done?" she asked. "Yeah . . . I'm done."

The great thing about skiing is that you've got plenty of time for introspection. "So this is it. I'm a Democrat," weighed on my mind as I headed down the slopes. As time passed, however, I started to get comfortable with the idea. Clearly the modern day Democratic Party was the party of fiscal and social responsibility. Like a physician, the motto of the Democratic party seemed to be "do no harm." Like a good fiscal conservative, the philosophy of the party seemed to be allowing a well-regulated free market to run its course. With no intrusion into moral matters.

Dad's Not Going to Like This

Despite my growing enthusiasm, there was one person I knew would be less than thrilled by my new party affiliation—my dad. We had never had a political disagreement. I had walked side by side with him, holding up the Limbaugh Banner of Truth. This wasn't going to be easy. I started running through permutations of the things he would say when he found out, and how I would respond.

I decided the direct approach would be best. I'd just come right out and say, "Dad . . . I'm a liberal." I half considered buying one of those "coming out to your family" books, because that's what it felt like. In fact, it might've been easier for my parents to accept me if I had been gay. At least somewhere in the back of their minds they could dismiss that as "the way God made me." But alas, I was fated to be liberal, and if ever there was an alternative lifestyle choice, it's the decision to become a liberal.

I didn't want to wait until we got home from our trip to tell my dad. So I decided to call him while Becky and I were waiting for our flight in Denver. That way he could know the truth, think about it, and come to terms with it. That way much of the initial nastiness would ebb from his system, and I'd be dealing with a more rational person when I got back. I dialed . . .

"Hello?"

"Hey dad, it's me."

"Hey."

"Dad . . . I want to tell you something . . . "

"Really, me too! I just found out I'm going to have heart surgery."

"WHAT? Oh my God. . . . When?"

"Next month. I'll need you to help out."

"Yeah, sure, Dad. Whatever you need me to do!"

"Thanks, son. I'll see you when you get back."

"See you soon, Dad!"

[*Click*]

So much for my big announcement. He was having heart problems, and finding out his son was a "flaming lib" would've killed him for sure!

Fortunately, the surgery went well—no complications, and he recovered faster than any of us dared hope. Still, even after his surgery, I felt that I couldn't tell my dad the truth and risk upsetting his recovery. The only answer was to stay in the closet. And this wasn't going to be an easy secret to keep. I was a liberal, and my former Republican Party disgusted me. Plus, it was a presidential election year.

Outing Myself on the Radio

True to form, the Republican Party had their strategy mapped out no matter who the Democrats ran in 2004. "Dean's crazy! Edwards is a rube! Clark is Clinton's boy! Kerry's a flip-flopper!" It was clear to me that for the duration of the 2004 election cycle, every dittohead would temporarily morph into a dittiot.

But rather than let it get to me, I decided it would be more useful to study the dittiot in his native habitat. Be an impartial (okay, semipartial) observer. Take notes. Remember what it had been like to be in their shoes. And in some small way maybe even try to help them find a way out of it.

My observations began during the Democratic Convention, where in the absence of anything remotely resembling negativity against the president, the right-wing media went to work personally attacking Kerry. (Remember "Swift Boat Veterans for Truth"?) However, it was nothing compared to what came out of the Republican Convention. The term "flip-flop" would be used thousands of times during the convention's three days, while Osama bin Laden would be mentioned only once. And Democrats got the rap of having no plan for the future?

Things got especially contentious for me after the Republican Convention. There is a local right-wing talk show host here in Memphis named Mike Fleming. As with Sean Hannity, I didn't like Mike all that much even when I agreed with him, but I had never had much of an incentive to respond to him. Now that I was batting for the other team, the urge to fight back took over.

I had first taken issue with Mike via email over a local issue, and he responded by calling me an idiot and saying I didn't know what I was talking about. When I responded with facts that illustrated the truth of what I was saying, Mike called me an idiot again, but this time only in the sense that all liberals are idiots. At no point did he argue the substance of what I was saying, so it was somewhat surprising when he invited me to his studio to talk face to face.

In person he was much different from the guy he was on the air. We both talked about our convictions and where they came from, and surprisingly, I found him to be immensely respectable as a person. I just thought that, politically, he was full of crap.

A couple of months later Mike asked me to be a guest on his show. Despite the fact that some of my friends would be listening, I knew my dad didn't listen to Mike Fleming, so I wasn't worried about "outing" myself on the radio.

Being on Mike's show was a mixed bag. On one hand, it was frustrating to face the same cognitive dissonance I used to embody—it was like arguing with my former self. Any mainstream media source had to be a lie and any right-wing media source had to be the truth. On the other hand, I enjoyed landing a few haymakers, and sticking up for the first Democratic candidate I ever supported, John Kerry.

During the election, the right liked to presume that John Kerry had had mad political ambitions that led him to volunteer for service in Vietnam. As absurd statements go, this one ranks right up there with "the Earth is flat" and "the moon is made of cheese." I thought it more likely that Kerry volunteered out of a sense of patriotism.

Reason be damned, right-wingers insisted that Kerry's having brought an 8mm handicam with him to Vietnam was somehow proof of his phony and ambitious nature. I thought this didn't make a lick of sense. So when Mike asked me, "Why else would he have brought a camera to Vietnam?" I responded, "My parents gave me a video camera to take with me to college in Knoxville. It's not uncommon for kids to have a camera with them during their college years!" Mike was unimpressed. "There's a big difference between Knoxville and Vietnam, Jim." To which I replied, "You're right, Mike! There's a hell of a lot more stuff to see in Vietnam!" We went to commercial. When we came back, Mike changed the subject. I put that one down as a win.

The most bizarre (and funniest) moment came during the discussion of Kerry's voting record. Mike, like most dittiots at the time, kept pointing to John Kerry's votes on omnibus Senate bills as proof of Kerry's hatred of the military. This rankled me on a lot of different levels. First, the programs Kerry voted to cut were the same programs that Dick Cheney said we didn't need when he was secretary of defense. So this one seemed a bit intellectually dishonest as a criticism. But my main point was that I didn't think it was appropriate to compare Kerry's votes from the '80s to today's world. This ties back to my principle that if everything changed after 9/11, everything was different before then as well. I tried to explain this to Mike, saying, "I don't think it's fair to base your decisions today on what someone was doing 25 years ago." Mike disagreed. "Oh, you absolutely *have* to look at what someone was doing 25 years ago!" he exclaimed. Then it occurred to me, "Well if that's the case, President Bush was driving drunk 25 years ago. Shouldn't *that* factor into your decision-making process?"

Mike quickly went to a caller, and while the caller was asking her question, Mike went off the air to admonish me. "That really was low, Jim! I can't believe you'd resort to that kind of personal attack." I was flabbergasted. Mike and his ilk were spending all day every day in every form of media calling decorated Vietnam veteran John Kerry a coward and a liar, and I point out, using Mike's own logic, how Bush's 25-year-old DUI is relevant, and somehow *I've* gone beyond the pale?

After the show was over, Mike and I were walking to our cars, and he was still badgering me about the DUI comment. I explained that it was *his* ground rule, and I didn't see what was unfair about what I had said. Mike's response said everything you need to know about the right-wing media. "You can't compare a 25-year Senate record to a DUI!" At last something we agreed on. "You're right, Mike. You can't compare a 25-year Senate record to a DUI." Mike seemed pleased. "Okay then. As long as we're in agreement," he said. I left, shaking my head in disbelief.

Why Were YOU Listening?

I got into my car and turned my cell phone back on. I had 10 new voicemail messages, presumably from friends who had listened to the show. I dialed into my voicemail.

"Well, this is your father! I can't believe my son is a pinko liberal! [*Laughter*] Call me when you get off the air."

My heart practically stopped. What was he doing listening to Mike! He never listened to Mike! His laugh told me he wasn't outraged or anything—merely surprised. I had just outed myself on the radio.

Fortunately my relationship with my father hasn't changed as a result. But with the full benefit of hindsight, I understand why it was a mistake for me to stay in the closet for so long. To my dad, my change from Republican to Democrat was quite literally overnight. I had never shared any of the thousand cuts with him along the way, and you can't just spring this momentous a change on someone all at once. As a result, my dad thinks my transformation was the result of outside forces, and not a change that occurred from within. Today we have conversations as though I've been a lifelong liberal, which is unfortunate. If I had shared this journey with him as it happened to me, he might have a greater understanding of where I'm coming from. To a large extent, that's why I wrote this book.

PART II
THE DITTOHEAD BRAIN

•

It's time to get tactical. Enough about "framing" and "memes" and "getting our message out there." That gives the right way too much credit for what they do. Think of the dittohead mind as an engine that's out of tune. We can bash it with a hammer, but aside from being cathartic, it's not going to help the engine run any better. What I want to do is show you how the engine works, how it got out of tune, and what we need to do to fix it.

In Part II, I am going to provide insight into how the dittohead brain reacts to the major political and social issues of the day in order to show how dittoheads think, and what liberals and progressives can do to try and change that thinking. Be aware that there is no magic word or phrase or line of reasoning that you can use to shake someone out of their dittohead-ism. It has to happen on its own. But that's not to say there aren't things you can do to expedite the process. If you feed a dittohead a steady, non-threatening dose of reality, it may eventually change their worldview lens.

11 : YOU CAN LEAD A DITTOHEAD TO KNOWLEDGE, BUT YOU CAN'T MAKE HIM THINK

●

One of the most frustrating aspects of dealing with dittoheads is the way they casually dismiss facts that are counter to their worldview. However, you have to realize that the right-wing mindset is a pretty deep rabbit hole. It's been carefully programmed over the last decade or two to respond in a predictable manner to various stimuli. What makes "them" different from "us" is that their core issues radiate from a central point, like the fingers on a hand. Social, fiscal, religious, and military policy all revolve around the concept that conservatives are right, and everyone else is wrong. When conservatives get organized, they can curl this hand into a fist . . . with which they've been pummeling liberals for years. Every now and then, liberals try to lob a volleyball of truth back at them, and dittoheads use that fist to smack it right back in their faces.

By contrast, the core issues that are important to liberals

exist more as independent entities. Fiscal progressives don't necessarily get all worked up about the environment, and social progressives don't make a whole lot of fuss when it comes to the budget. So compared to the conservative "hand," liberals are more like a series of separate pieces: a finger, a thumb, etc. Each may be very good at doing what it does, but they're not very effective weapons because they aren't often used in combination.

Inside the Dittiot Mind

One mistake liberals often make is thinking that Republicans are not intelligent. They assume that their detachment from reality is due to some form of functional mental retardation. But Republicans are just as intelligent as liberals. The main difference is the elective surgery performed by the conservative media, which installs a "right-wing reasoning chip" that surrounds the "worldview" portion of the Republican brain. Its primary purpose is to apply a pass/fail test to any incoming information. This is important because the "worldview" portion is upstream from the "critical thinking" portion of the brain. If information can't get past "worldview," then it has to take a long and perilous journey through the "soul search" mountains to get to "critical thinking." Rarely does information survive such a journey. The secondary function of the chip is to project a negative image on those who disagree with it. For example, "I think the sky is blue, therefore liberals think the sky is red."

Let me break it down and show you how it works. Let's say you, as a liberal, tell your dittohead friend that we haven't found any WMDs in Iraq. That information moves along the dittohead brain until it hits the "right-wing reasoning chip," which checks the brain's worldview to see if the information is compatible. The worldview replies "no." Therefore the information must be faulty. The chip then sends a reply to the mouth: "Where'd you hear that?" There are three possible answers to this question, and all three satisfy the chip's need for denial.

Answer #1: "I heard it on the news."
Chip's Response: "You can't trust anything the liberal media says. Information = False"

Answer #2: "It was in the Duelfer Report."
Chip's Response: "Rush said the Duelfer Report justified the war in Iraq. The liberal media is lying about the information in the report. Information = False"

Answer #3: "Bush said it last night on TV."
Chip's Response: "You're talking to a liberal. Liberals lie. Information = False"

Trust me when I say that the "right-wing reasoning chip" has an answer that can deny anything counter to its worldview.

The PIPA Study—The Gift That Keeps on Giving

To see the chip perform some real acrobatics, let's take a look at what I can only describe as the greatest liberal Christmas present ever to dittoheads—the PIPA Study. For those of you who are unfamiliar with it, PIPA stands for the Program on International Policy Attitudes. It was a joint project between the Center on Policy Attitudes and the Center for International and Security

Studies at the University of Maryland. On October 21, 2004, PIPA released the results of a polling study regarding Bush and Kerry supporters' views on a variety of issues, appropriately entitled "The Separate Realities of Bush and Kerry Supporters."

One question asked in the study was, "Is it your belief that, just before the war, Iraq had actual weapons of mass destruction?"[1] Bush supporters said yes to the tune of 47 percent, versus Kerry supporters, who voted in the affirmative at 8 percent. An additional 25 percent of Bush supporters believed that even though Saddam didn't have WMDs, he had a major program in place to develop them (versus 18 percent of Kerry supporters). Surely this is hardly worth mentioning, as *everyone* thought Saddam had WMDs before the war, right? But here's what's remarkable—this study was conducted *after* the Duelfer Report was released.

Iraq had no WMDs when we invaded. In fact, Iraq hadn't had a stockpile of WMDs since 1998. The only things we were able to find were bits and pieces of Saddam's old program. He may have hoped to revive the program at some point in the future, but he wasn't going to do so as long as UN sanctions were in place.

A rational person would look at the findings of the Duelfer Report and draw one conclusion: The sanctions were working. We could have used the international community as leverage, and likely could have forced an eventual regime change in Iraq without resorting to a go-it-alone war. There was no immediate danger; therefore the rush (as in "hurry," not "chubby addict") to war was completely unnecessary.

Even the right-wing reasoning chip might have come to that

conclusion if it didn't receive some emergency reprogramming. The day the Duelfer Report came out, Rush went on the air, saying, "This totally justifies our going to war with Iraq. It confirms everything we knew to be true before we invaded!" The rest of the right-wing media followed suit. The chip was appeased. Besides, the Duelfer Report is over a 1,000 pages long. Who had time to read it? Instead, dittoheads say, "I'll just accept what Rush says, because I'm not going to read the report, and what he is saying is exactly what I want to hear anyway."

Back to the PIPA study. Another question asked was, "Did the Duelfer Report conclude that Iraq had WMDs, or at least a major program for developing them?"[2] This wasn't a "what do you think" question, this was a "what do you know" question. A majority of Bush supporters (57 percent) said yes, that was the conclusion of the report, as opposed to 23 percent of Kerry supporters. It's one thing to believe something *in spite* of proof to the contrary, but it's quite another to believe something *because* of it.

The study also asked respondents to categorize the relationship between Iraq and Al Qaeda. A whopping 75 percent of Bush supporters believed Iraq gave substantial support to Al Qaeda, or that Iraq was directly involved in carrying out the 9/11 attacks (55 percent and 20 percent, respectively).[3] The same respondents were asked if the 9/11 Commission Report had found clear evidence that Iraq had substantial collaborative ties to 9/11, and 56 percent said yes, despite the fact that it wasn't true.[4]

Maybe the whole WMD thing just didn't matter to Bush supporters. Maybe they would have supported the war for whatever reason Bush dreamed up, and the fact that they had been deceived was irrelevant. The PIPA folks thought of that. They asked, if prewar intelligence indicated that Iraq had no substantive ties to Al Qaeda and no WMDs, should we have gone to war anyway? A whopping 58 percent of Bush supporters said "no, we shouldn't have gone to war."[5]

That's why this whole exercise is so important. It did matter to Bush supporters whether or not Iraq had WMDs or ties to Al Qaeda (though not as much as it mattered to Kerry supporters, 92 percent of whom were against going to war if no WMDs or Iraq-Al Qaeda connection were found). If Bush supporters had known the truth before the election, it seems like many of them wouldn't have voted for him. But the administration and the right-wing media were able to muddy the waters so that the average Republican voter just didn't know what to believe anymore, and that kind of situation very much favors the incumbent. Better the devil you know than the devil you don't.

Someone to Blame

With all the pre- and postwar screw-ups, how could the average dittohead not blame the Republicans? Very simple—blame the Democrats instead! Here's how the right-wing reasoning chip worked out all the cognitive dissonance:

"Saddam planned to start up his weapons program once sanctions were lifted."

"I support the war in Iraq, therefore liberals must oppose it."

"The opposite of war is peace, meaning the opposite of war with Iraq must be 'lifting sanctions.'"

"If liberals had their way, Saddam would have resumed his WMD program."

"Therefore thank God Bush invaded Iraq when he did, or

liberals would have given him the bomb just like they did with China. (Don't ask. It's a whole other thing.)"

"The liberal media's interpretation of the Duelfer Report is obviously just an attempt to cover up the fact that they were wrong, just like they always are."

See how effortless that was? Step 1: Project the opposite of my worldview on liberals—"I believe in going to war, so liberals must believe in lifting sanctions." Step 2: Keep twisting dissonant information until you can figure out a way to make it fit your worldview. Step 3: Anything that still doesn't make sense can be attributed to "liberal bias." And voilà, an impenetrable wall has been erected between "worldview" and "critical thought." "Nothing I disagree with is getting by here!" the chip says.

If you want to be successful with dittoheads, you've got to be ready to force-feed them the truth. They'll kick and scream and holler if you're not careful. But if you use the right set of numbers from the right source, sometimes you can overload the chip, and then you can feed information directly into the critical-thought portion of the brain. And that's how you can win!

12 : HOW TO TALK TO A DITTOHEAD (AND YOU MUST!)

•

Have you ever see the game Plinko on the TV show *The Price Is Right?* If you haven't, the way it works is that contestants drop discs the size of small Frisbees along the top of a large board, then watch as these discs bounce their way down the board. Along the bottom of the board are slots with dollar amounts ranging from as little as $100 to as much as $10,000. You take home whatever dollar amount your chips land on. However, not all of the slots pay off. On either side of the $10,000 slot, for example, are $0 slots, so if you just go for the big prize, you often end up with nothing.

Plinko is the perfect parallel to how it is to argue with a dittohead. Whenever you start a conversation with a dittohead, you're picking a spot along the top of the board to drop your chip. The dittohead will then do everything in his or her power to filter that chip into one of the $0 slots. If you always try to hit the $10,000 hopper, you will wind up going home empty-handed.

You'll know that you've hit an empty slot if you hear any one of the following statements during the course of your conversation:

"Your answer to everything is raise taxes."

"You're just another big-government, tax-and-spend liberal."

"And you believe what you hear from the liberal media?"

"You just hate Bush."

"Yeah, but that was Clinton's fault." (or, "Clinton didn't do anything about it, either.")

"Don't you think 9/11 had something to do with that?" (or, "9/11 changed everything!")

"You're one of those 'Blame America First' types!"

"Yeah, but both sides do it!"

And finally, when all else fails: "Let's just agree to disagree."

Remember, the right-wing reasoning chip has been well-conditioned by Rush and the rest of the right-wing media to resist all arguments from liberals. This is what makes conversing with dittoheads such an uphill battle—Rush and his ilk have defined for them what it means to be a Democrat and a liberal, eliminating the need for dittoheads to find out anything on their own.

Most fans of Rush have developed what they like to call the "big picture." You'll hear them use this phrase whenever you point out something that Rush either got wrong or flat out made up. "Well, maybe he got that wrong, but he's still right about the big picture." Part of the "big picture" includes the working definition of "liberals."

As the emergence of the term "progressive" illustrates, Rush and company have done a great job turning the word "liberal" into a pejorative term. So much so that for most conservatives, "liberal" is the new "ni**er." You can see this illustrated by replacing the word "liberal" with the n-word in the titles of conservative books, and seeing that the spirit is the same with the new word in place. For example—*Deliver Us from Evil: Saving the World from Terrorism, Despotism, and Liberalism*; *How to Talk to a Liberal (If You Must)*; and my personal favorite, Thomas Sowell's *Black Rednecks and White Liberals.*

So realize that, in an argument with a dittohead, you'll rarely, if ever, hit the big prize in one shot. You're better off trying to hit those little $300 and $500 slots on the side. Instead of trying to change the world during your lunch hour, try to get small compromises. The dittohead mindset is quite literally the elephant you have to eat one bite at a time. It's a lot like chess. You have to visualize where you want to end up.

The One Thing You Should Never Say

Since the dittohead vision of a liberal is as an angry, Bush-hating, anti-American wacko, there is one surefire thing you can say that will immediately confirm this stereotype to them and end any shot you may have had at reasonable discourse.

"Bush is a liar."

Believe me, I know that this is the hardest one for liberals to keep to themselves, but it's important that you never, ever say it to a dittohead. Remember, dittoheads view liberals as a homogeneous group who all believe the same thing and behave the same way. (Much the same way that many liberals view dittoheads.) If you use language consistent with what they perceive your beliefs to be when talking to them, nothing's going to get through no matter how true it may be. And since liberals have been defined as angry, Bush-hating wackos, in their minds, calling Bush a liar immediately satisfies all three stereotypes.

There is good news, however—you don't need to call Bush a liar in order to make your point. First off, let's deal with reality—we will never know what Bush did or did not know prior to the Iraq war. Calling him a liar implies that we have some definitive proof as to Bush's intentions. Like it or not, we don't. It is conceivable, however unlikely, that Bush really did do what he thought was right in Iraq based on the intelligence he had at the time. Sure, that intelligence was flawed, there was clearly intelligence to the contrary, and Cheney & Co. had an anti-Saddam agenda long before 9/11. And, yeah, all those things put together make Bush look pretty bad. But the only thing that they prove definitively is that Bush is a lousy boss.

So instead of hopping up and down and holding your breath screaming that Bush is a liar (which we can't prove and no dittohead will ever agree with anyway), why not just say what we all can agree on—that Bush is a lousy chief executive? That he's just not good at his job. Start from there and you'll be able to make inroads with dittoheads. You can point to Bush's cronyism, or his "big-government" brand of conservatism, or his inability to get his policies implemented with majorities in all branches of government as evidence that he's a bad boss. You'll be surprised to find that most dittoheads will agree with you!

13 : SILENCING THE BIG GUN OF PERSONAL RESPONSIBILITY

•

The number-one overriding principle of conservatism is personal responsibility. Republicans believe in holding people accountable for their actions (though right now they're only willing to
hold Democrats responsible), while at the same time saying that
those who believe that *anything* could be responsible for failure
are making excuses. In short, you should be able to "overcome"
all obstacles on your own, by hard work, and certainly without
the government's help.

Some call this philosophy "Social Darwinism," whereby only
the economically strong survive. While it is interesting to watch
dittoheads writhe when you ask why "Social Darwinism" is okay,
but "Biological Darwinism" is not, I have a slightly different take
on the shortcomings of the Republican mantra of "personal
responsibility," which you may be able to make use of when
explaining to your dittohead friends why government is not

always the enemy. First, however, let's talk about an issue that has always been endemic to the Republican Party—racism—so that we can understand why it undermines their notion of personal responsibility.

The Soft Racism of Personal Responsibility

Republicans don't subscribe to the same notion of racism as the rest of us. If the individual can overcome any obstacle, then it's the individual's fault when he or she fails. African-Americans make less money than their white counterparts because they fail as individuals. Hispanics working for less than minimum wage fail because they won't take responsibility for themselves. The Americans with Disabilities Act is unnecessary, because if wheelchair-ridden people *really* wanted that job they'd *find* a way to get up those stairs.

Dittoheads bristle when people call them racists—not because they're embarrassed to be called racist, but because they think racism is really "excuse-ism." Rush and other conservative luminaries have described this as the "soft racism of low expectations." People are expected to be able to overcome racism on their own if it does exist, or quit blaming other people for their failures if it doesn't. Like many Republican beliefs, it's a neatly closed circle. And best of all, it leaves you without an obligation to help anybody.

I agree with Martin Luther King, Jr., who defined racism as judging someone by the color of their skin, not the content of their character. That's why I think it's racist when someone spends three hours a day on the radio stereotyping virtually all aspects of modern-day black culture, society, and leadership.

Every time someone says rap music is devoid of socially redeeming features, a racist stereotype has been made. Every time it's said that the number of children born out of wedlock is endemic of black culture in general, a racist stereotype has been made. Every time Rush calls NBA players "NBA thugs," a racist stereotype has been made. Many dittoheads will say, "But it's not a stereotype if it's true," which creates yet another racist stereotype.

Pot, Have You Met Kettle?

Speaking of Rush, you can almost see him flinch (even on the radio) when he uses the "r" word, and for good reason—he knows there's no way in hell he should be able to get away with calling anyone a racist. Not after Donovan McNabb. Remember when Rush said the only reason McNabb got so much attention was because the liberal sports media wanted to see a black do well? When Rush made that comment, McNabb had just started in his third Pro Bowl, had taken his team to two straight NFC Championship games, and had been the runner-up for the Most Valuable Player award in his first year as a starter.

As an isolated incident, it would be unfair to assume anything about Rush's stance on racism from the McNabb comment. Unfortunately for Rush, the McNabb comment isn't an isolated incident. When he was starting his broadcasting career, he once asked a black caller to "take that bone out of your nose and call me back" so that he could understand what he was saying. Rush more or less apologized for this in a 1990 *Newsday* article by saying he felt guilty for having said it.[1] (Guilt is as close to an apology as you're going to get out of Rush.) But he didn't feel guilty about another line he used at the time: "Have you ever noticed how all newspaper composite pictures of wanted criminals resemble Jesse Jackson?" [2]

Would you like a more contemporary example? On July 14, 2005, Republican National Committee Chair Ken Mehlman addressed the NAACP to say that the GOP regretted the "Southern Strategy" it had used during the Nixon administration. If you are unaware, the Southern Strategy was the right's plan to court Southern white Democrats who were upset about the civil rights movement. It is widely regarded that this attempt to profit from racism is what cost the party of Lincoln the support of the black community. In a simple gesture of reconciliation, Mehlman said, "We can't call ourselves a true majority unless we reach out to African-Americans . . . there was a time when African-American support turned Democrat, and we didn't do enough to retain it." [3]

You wouldn't think there was anything in Mehlman's remarks to get all bent out of shape about. Rush disagreed. "Know what he's going to do? He's going to go down there and basically apologize for what has come to be known as the Southern Strategy. . . . He's going to go down there and apologize for it. In the midst of all of this, in the midst of all that's going on [terrorism, Iraq, the Supreme Court, etc.], once again, Republicans are going to go bend over and grab the ankles." [4]

However, Rush didn't stop there, instead turning the tables to accuse *others* of racism. You don't think Condi's doing her job? That's racist! You think we're failing in Iraq? That's racist! You're opposing Bush's Hispanic court nominees? That's racist! You want to keep Social Security the way it is? That's racist!

This is how Republicans approach racism. If they repeat it enough, if Rush and the right-wing media repeat the word "racist" over and over again, assigning it to *everything*, then it will lose its meaning for *anything*. And then the average Joe will just throw up his hands and say "Gee, what does racism even mean?"

Ann Coulter—Heel Wrestler

Maybe I'm being unfair. Maybe conservatives really are serious about racism. Maybe it's just Rush who has some "issues." Maybe. . . . But then I read something like Ann Coulter's December 9, 2004 piece, "The New and Improved Racism," and I'm reminded of the title to Charles Barkley's autobiography—*I May Be Wrong . . . But I Doubt It.*

Coulter argues that opposition to any minority for any reason is racist. It's the color of the skin, not the content of the character that you should judge. Here are some excerpts:

> "Still furious about the election, liberals are lashing out at blacks. First it was Condoleezza Rice. But calling a Ph.D. who advised a sitting president during war 'Aunt Jemima' apparently hasn't satiated the Democrats' rage."[5]

Now, *maybe* Ann would have a point if Howard Dean or Barbara Boxer or some other prominent Democrat called Condi an "Aunt Jemima." But the "Aunt Jemima" comment was made by John "Sly" Sylvester.[6] No, I haven't heard of him either, but just in case you were wondering, Mr. Sylvester has (or had) a morning talk show in Madison, Wisconsin. I suppose I could mention that at around the same time, another obscure right-wing radio talk-show host, Mark Bellings, referred to Mexicans as "wet-backs."[7] But that's just creating an equivalency, making it sound like I'm trying to muddy the waters by saying both sides do it. I'd rather call both guys idiots, and say that neither is indicative of the prevailing wisdom in either party.

Back to Ann:

> " . . . last Sunday Harry Reid, the Democratic leader in the Senate, had this to say about Justice Clarence Thomas: 'I think that he has been an embarrassment to the Supreme Court. I think that his opinions are poorly written.' You'd think Thomas' opinions were written in ebonics."[8]

When I was in college my business law professor told my class that Justice Thomas did a poor job of writing judicial opinions. I was outraged at the time, and chalked up my professor's opinion to his clear liberal bias. When I confronted him after class, he listened to my complaints without saying a word. Then he reached into his wallet and took out his Republican National Committee membership card. "I'm a Republican," he said. "And Justice Thomas writes poor judicial opinions."

What matters to Coulter is the color of the person's skin, not their ability to do their job.

Beyond just being hypocritical, Coulter's article is also note-worthy because she's the one on point for the Republicans. Ann's kind of like a "heel" wrestler. At first, everyone boos her and throws stuff in the ring. That's called "heel heat." It's the equivalent of jeering for the bad guy. But if the heel keeps doing the same stuff month after month, people stop caring. The boos diminish, and the heel has to do more and more outrageous stuff to keep getting heat. Eventually the crowd decides they don't care anymore. They don't boo. They don't react. They just patiently wait for the heel to go away so the show can continue. That's where we are with Ann Coulter.

But this all serves a purpose—to desensitize. Coulter says something outrageous ("Democrats are racist") and takes all the flack. Dems respond, saying "This is absurd! We demand an apology." And once someone like Ann Coulter opens the door, the rest of the right-wing media can go right through, having had the way before them cleared. "Oh, so it's okay to call Condi an Aunt Jemima," Rush or Sean Hannity or some other conservative media type points out, "but if we point out how you hate a black guy you get all bent out of shape. Democrats can dish it out, but they can't take it." And the average Joe is left confused, wondering if maybe Democrats *are* racists?

Hurricane Katrina

Nowhere has this soft racism of personal responsibility been more evident than with the right's reaction to Hurricane Katrina. As thousands of African-Americans were left to fend for themselves for the better part of a week, right-wing pundits were asking things such as, "Why didn't those people just get out of there when they had the chance?" They couldn't understand why impoverished African-Americans didn't just load up the Infiniti SUV with a week's worth of Perrier and Powerbars and head to their summer homes in Aspen. Rick Santorum went so far as to suggest that those who stayed behind should be made to pay some sort of fine for all the trouble they'd caused.

Then, when Bush started throwing around the dollar amounts that he said he would spend in the rebuilding effort, conservatives bristled, asking why New Orleans couldn't pay for its own reconstruction, or even asking why it had to be rebuilt at all.

This was personal responsibility in action, and it showed the clear difference between Republican and Democratic ideology. Democrats believe that the role of government is to help those who can't help themselves, like, say, poor people stranded hip-deep in a toxic gumbo. Republicans looked at the same tragedy and said, "Let's get out of the way and let the private sector do its job." However, the private sector doesn't make a habit out of helping people with no money.

Beyond issues of race and class, Katrina exposed what I think is the core fallacy in the dittohead mindset: the idea that personal responsibility and government are mutually exclusive. That if the government is involved in something, it's only to give away money or resources, which will lead to a "dependency class" that will become incapable of fending for itself.

Dittoheads are fond of asking questions like, "How has the government ever helped anybody? Name one person who became successful because of the government." I can name that person: my grandfather, Jack Behringer.

My grandfather is not what you would call a government freeloader. In fact, if anything, he perfectly exemplifies the Republican ideal of making things happen for oneself. He was an immigrant child who grew up during the Great Depression. His family sacrificed every day to make ends meet. As a member of the Greatest Generation, he served in the Army in the Pacific Theater of World War II as a radio operator.

Upon returning from the war, he went to college thanks to the G.I. Bill. Upon graduation he went to work for the F.B.I., where he spent his entire career, marrying his sweetheart, putting four daughters through college, and being a fabulous grandfather to eight grandchildren. The pension he earned afforded him a comfortable (but not lavish) retirement.

Everything my grandfather has he earned through his own blood, sweat, and tears. And at the same time, everything my grandfather has, he has because of the government. When it works the right way, government doesn't deny personal responsibility—it multiplies it every bit as much as dittoheads say the private sector does. The government put my grandfather through college and paid for my mother's education, which led to her meeting my father. Hell, now that I think about it, government is probably the reason why I'm here!

My grandfather's story is one that combines the notion of good liberal government with the concept of personal responsibility, with the best possible outcome. Think of that the next time a dittohead asks, "What has the government ever done for anybody?"

14 : THE WEAK FAITH OF THE RELIGIOUS RIGHT

•

Have you ever seen the picture where, if you look at it one way, you see a beautiful young woman, but if you look at it another way, you see an old hag? This is a great analogy when it comes to the very public religion of dittoheads. Where they see a beautiful young lady of traditional values, we liberals see the ugly hag of legislated morality. But, since we're both looking at the same picture, elements of both views are present, depending on how you look at it.

With ample help from Rush, most dittoheads live in fear of the "secular left"—a powerful cabal of runaway liberal judges who seek to make America an atheist nation. From that perspective, what they do makes sense, as the dittohead nation believes it is fighting for the very future of Christianity. To them, Jesus is the beautiful lady in the picture.

To liberals, the ugly hag is the dittoheads' insistence on official, public acknowledgement of their religion. It's not enough that dittoheads have faith themselves, or that they're good people, or that they give to their church. It goes beyond that. Everyone else has to admit that their way is the right way, the only way. Every issue radiates out from this—prayer in schools, *Roe v. Wade*, assisted suicide, evolution, gay marriage, etc. Dittoheads repeat the same refrain over and over again—"We're right, you're wrong, so let's legislate accordingly."

However, one of the great ironies of religious dittoheadism is that they already have everything they say they want. They want prayer in schools? Well, in most states there is a mandated moment of silence during the school day in which kids are free to pray silently. (That's the key word that dittoheads hate: "silently.") I prayed every morning when I was in high school, and I was never suspended or harassed for it.

They say they want stickers on science textbooks warning about the dangers of evolution. Well, if a family doesn't believe in evolution, they're free to tell their kids, "Some people believe in evolution, but we don't." And if you want your child's education to be based in the Bible, you can send him to a private school or even opt for homeschooling.

Dittoheads say they don't want schools teaching their kids anything but abstinence when it comes to sex ed. But they can hold their kids out of sex-ed classes if they don't want them exposed to anything other than abstinence-based instruction.

But despite all this, dittoheads still believe that they need to fight back against the imaginary boogeyman of the "secular left." Sure, their kids can pray in school, they say, but they can't form a prayer clique during school hours. They worry that if their kids even hear the word "evolution," it will cause them to abandon Christ. And if their kids catch wind of anything other than abstinence, they'll be having unprotected teenage sex all over the place.

I find all of this to represent a startlingly weak faith. To believe that your kids will turn away from God unless He has been officially sanctioned by the government? Do the Ten Commandments have to be sanctioned by the government before you can consider them valid? And what happened to the dittohead mantra of personal responsibility? Isn't it ultimately the parents' responsibility to make sure their kids are brought up right?

These are the kinds of questions we should be asking dittoheads. Instead we say nothing, trying to be "reasonable" and not make it sound like we're questioning anyone's religious beliefs. But that's not what this debate is about. Ultimately, what drives the dittoheads' desire for legislation is the need to protect people from behavior that they consider self-destructive. Or to put it another way, they think we need laws to protect people from themselves.

Thou Shalt Not Take the Founding Fathers' Names in Vain

We could choose any number of things to illustrate dittohead outrage, but what encapsulates it best is the Ten Commandments debate. On many an occasion Rush has perpetuated the myth that this country was founded by Christians, and that the founding fathers never intended for church and state to be separated. But even a cursory glance at some quotes from the founding fathers indicates otherwise:

"The government of the United States is not in any sense founded on the Christian religion." **John Adams, from the Treaty of Tripoli, Article 11**

"One day the dawn of reason and freedom of thought in the United States will tear down the artificial scaffolding of Christianity. And the day will come when the mystical generation of Jesus, by the Supreme Being as His father, in the womb of a virgin will be classed with the fable of the generation of Minerva in the brain of Jupiter." **Thomas Jefferson, from a letter to John Adams, April 11, 1823**

"Some books against Deism fell into my hands. . . . It happened that they wrought an effect on me quite contrary to what was intended by them; for the arguments of the Deists, which were quoted to be refuted, appeared to me much stronger than the refutations, in short, I soon became a thorough Deist." **Benjamin Franklin,** *The Autobiography of Benjamin Franklin*

"Denominated a Deist, the reality of which I have never disputed, being conscious that I am no Christian." **Ethan Allen,** *Religion of the American Enlightenment*

"My own mind is my own church. All national institutions of churches, whether Jewish, Christian or Turkish, appear to me no other than human inventions, set up to terrify and enslave mankind, and monopolize power and profit." **Thomas Paine,** *The Age of Reason*

"The Civil Government, though bereft of everything like an associated hierarchy, possesses the requisite stability and performs its functions with complete success, whilst the number, the industry, and the morality of the priesthood, and the devotion of the people have been manifestly increased by the total separation of the Church from the State." **James Madison, from a letter to Robert Walsh, March 2, 1819**

In their own words the founding fathers said that ours was a nation established on the principle of freedom, not Christianity. Many of them didn't even believe in the divinity of Christ. Dittoheads have a hard time dealing with this, because they've been conditioned to view everything as a study in opposites—if someone doesn't believe in Christ, then they *have* to be an atheist. The idea of being a deist, for example, just doesn't compute, so they tune it out or ignore it entirely.

And, while it is true that the words "separation of church and state" do not appear in the Constitution, it is also noteworthy that the word "God" doesn't appear either. That's how seriously the founding fathers took the First Amendment. While many of them believed in God (even Thomas Paine, who is widely considered an atheist, wrote in *The Age of Reason* that he did believe in God and hoped to go to heaven), they didn't mention God in the document that founded their government. If that doesn't mean, "keep the Ten Commandments off the front lawn," I don't know what does.

That's why it's scary when I hear Antonin Scalia say that having the Ten Commandments in the courthouse acknowledges that our government ultimately derives its power from God.[1] Really? I kind of thought that our government derived its power from the "consent of the governed." It's a quick hop, skip and jump from God being the source of the government's power to God *powering* the government. From there springs all kinds of crazy things, like people saying "God chose the president." Or worse, the President could believe that he was chosen by God!

What Kind of Christian Would Jesus Be?

There are many practical reasons for wanting to keep church and state separated, many of which your average dittohead has probably never considered. Take this one for example: Whose religion do you teach in schools? Many Christians wrongly assume that they're all on the same side—"We all believe in Jesus as the Son of God." However, for contemporary Southern Baptists or Evangelicals, it's not enough to believe—you have to be born again. And that's just one difference between the *Christian* denominations; forget about the 20 percent of Americans who are religious "others."

Not that many dittoheads give a damn about the non-Christian minority, but the rest of us might want to consider being a little more farsighted. Someday Roman Catholicism might be the dominant religion in America. Do we want to establish a precedent that could lead to mandatory confession in schools? There's one sure way to make sure that doesn't happen, and that is to honor the founding fathers' intent in maximizing the distance between church and state. That's why a seemingly innocuous issue like the public display of the Ten Commandments is so important.

As with most issues facing us today, this is another one where we liberals are not on the wrong side—we're just losing the "framing war." If we let the right set the terms to the tune of "either you support the Ten Commandments or you hate God," then we lose. What we need to do is address the fundamental insecurity at the heart of the religious right's arguments. Why don't we try asking questions such as, "Why is your faith so weak that it can't exist without the government's approval?" Or better still, "Why won't you take personal responsibility for the religious education of your children?" It's kind of sad that we have to do this, but it may be the only way to get dittoheads to act in our—and their own—best interest. Using these arguments, plus the very words of the founding fathers, whom many dittoheads revere—think of the constitutional original-intent debate—may help your dittohead friend see the light. And for once, hopefully it won't be the light of God.

15 : THE EVOLUTION OF A WEDGE ISSUE

•

Back when I was learning the theory of evolution in high school, my biology teacher took great pains to tell us that not only was evolution just a *theory*, but that he himself did not subscribe to that theory. As a creationist, he explained that evolution couldn't be true because "the Earth is only 10,000 years old." When asked how he knew this, he responded, "Because the Bible says so." It was the first time someone suggested to me that God and science were mutually exclusive, and I had a hard time swallowing the idea. Though I was rather religious at the time, I didn't think that the Bible did well as a work of science. Even today, I believe the Bible remains "Zero for However-many-times-we've-said-the-Bible-is-right-and-science-is-wrong."

Science Is the Study of How God Works in the Universe

My wife and Thomas Paine helped me understand a lot about God. In *The Age of Reason*, Paine explained that when God supposedly tells man something directly, there is a lot of room for interpretation. Is pork really the meat of the Devil, or is it just kind of unsafe if you don't cook it right? Should you stand up and fight against the pharaoh, or just shut up and pay your taxes?

However, while the written word leaves lots of wiggle room for human judgment, there is one thing created by the hand of God that is not subject to human interpretation, and that's creation itself. That sentiment really changed the way I look at religion and science.

It took me forever to get this point, and I may have never reached it if it weren't for my wife and her cat. When we were dating, my wife tried to explain the transcendental notion of creation by saying that she saw the hand of God in the intricate patterns of her cat's fur. At the time I was still very much a dittohead (at one point while we were dating I accused her of blasphemy), and I dismissed the idea derisively. "You see God . . . in *cat hair?*" As with most things in my life, I would later discover she was right the whole time. I just wasn't in the right frame of mind to hear it or understand it.

If you accept the notion of a Gospel of Creation (which is really just saying that God created the universe, and it works the way He wants it to), then you shouldn't have a problem understanding that science is the process of understanding how God works in the universe.

This is one of my core principles, along with "The role of government is to help those who cannot help themselves."

Dittoheads don't get this. They see science as something that denies God. Episcopal Bishop John Shelby Spong, in *Why Christianity Must Change or Die,* explained that many religious people distrust science because they feel it moves God farther away from them. For example, we used to believe that God was in the clouds. Then we got up there and didn't find God. So we figured God must be on the other side of some celestial sphere that encased our solar system. Then we figured out there is no celestial sphere, etc., etc. As a result of science, we grew further and further removed from God.

Intelligent Design Doesn't Explain How YOU Got Here

I believe that an overwhelming majority of dittoheads are not biblical literalists. Most would agree that the Earth is millions of years old, and that dinosaurs and man didn't cohabitate the world at the same time. They're even willing to admit that evolution exists in the areas where they can't prove it doesn't. But when it comes to mankind and evolution, they believe that the past is simply prologue. That's where Intelligent Design takes over.

Intelligent Design teaches that there are two kinds of evolution—macroevolution and microevolution. Followers of ID (eerily similar to the "Monsters from the Id" from the sci-fi classic *Forbidden Planet*) will say they have no problem with the idea of microevolution. And there's a good reason for that: Microevolution is observable and scientifically provable. Since they can't prove that microevolution doesn't exist (because there's proof to the contrary), followers of ID instead draw the line at macroevolution, which is basically the idea that Monday's pond scum is Tuesday's Tom DeLay. Things don't change that quickly, they argue. Of course it is foolish to say that there can be small changes over thousands of years, but not big changes over millions of years. But for a lot of people that's just too big a chunk of time to fathom.

For dittoheads, it's a lot easier to accept *some* science by saying that God incubated the Earth for a couple million years, but then once he was done baking it, he put man on it 10,000 years ago (or thereabouts). Thus God remains mysterious and magical, and faith can be maintained. (It also gets rid of the uncomfortable idea that Africa was the "cradle of life" and allows for the belief that the first humans, Adam and Eve, were white. You know, like Jesus.) Best of all, evolution (a.k.a. microevolution) can still exist, but it only applies to "lesser organisms."

However, you can't very well say that evolution exists except for man, who came into being via the spontaneous will of God, and expect the scientific community to roll over and play dead. So the question remained: How to get this argument out into the mainstream? Having failed at replacing evolution with creationism, the right found a new answer in recent years: Create enough confusion over the theory of evolution so that it's just as believable as creationism, a role for which intelligent design is perfectly suited, in that it creates enough science for dittoheads to seem reasonable to the secular world, but not enough for them to have to give up their core beliefs.

I don't have any problem with folks believing in intelligent design. And if the issue were just one that my neighbor and I discussed over a beer, there wouldn't be a problem. But, of course, there is a problem. "Evolution vs. Intelligent Design" has become a political issue, and Rush and others have made it part of the right wing's larger war against the "secular left." It's not enough that I believe one thing and you believe another. As with most things in the dittohead universe, their view has to be publicly acknowledged as the only one.

I've Got Your Sticker Right Here

It especially rankles me to see elected leaders pretending to speak on God's behalf when they are in reality doing the opposite. An example of this is the textbook-sticker debate, which came to my own backyard in 2005, when a bill to put stickers on science textbooks was introduced by Memphis City School Councilman Wyatt Bunker. Here's the language of the proposed sticker:

> "This textbook contains material on scientific theories about creation. There are many scientific and religious theories about the nature and diversity of living things. All theories should be approached with an open mind, studied carefully and critically considered."

Rush is ardently "pro-sticker" and argues that language like this is innocuous. The problem in this case, however, was that the textbook itself said almost the exact same thing as the sticker when teaching the theory of evolution. In much the same way that the Federal Marriage Amendment is less about protecting marriage and more about "smiting gays," these stickers aren't meant to protect the fragile faith of our schoolchildren—they're meant to bring the church into the classroom. They're meant to distract, to create confusion, to blur the lines just enough for the right to get their agenda into the public schools—to create a scientific environment in which *their* idea of God can exist. This is not about teaching; it's about indoctrinating. It's the right trying to create yet another wedge issue by creating a false choice between God and science. Their point isn't to disprove evolution; it's to discredit it, to put forth a theory that you can't prove *or* disprove, but which will be palatable to mainstream Americans.

All of this goes back to the idea that unless God works by "magic," he doesn't exist. And evolution can't be true, since God would never choose to let his people come from some lesser species. (One of the primary objections to the theory of evolution is Christians' profound distaste in the notion of being descended from monkeys.) In addition to being a false choice, by my beliefs this is actually blasphemous. To deny science is to deny God.

This isn't going to be an easy argument to make to dittoheads. They are hardwired to accept God and science as mutually exclusive. And those who believe in science, like my high school biology teacher, are probably too far gone to be reasoned with. But with some hard work and a little common sense, I think we can get some of the more intelligently designed dittoheads to see the light, and to understand that they can have their science and their God too. Perhaps a line like this might work on them: "Personal responsibility is basically another way of saying that only the strong survive, so it should naturally follow that evolution is the ultimate triumph of personal responsibility!"

16: BEATING THE GAY DRUMHEAD

•

In the perfect dittohead world, gays wouldn't be allowed to marry or share assets with the people they love. They wouldn't be protected from discrimination at work or from hate crimes. They wouldn't be allowed to raise children. They would be granted the same medical visitation rights as perfect strangers. In short, gays would be second-class citizens.

As our culture became more and more accepting of the existence of homosexuality, the right-wing battle moved from being against gay people to fighting the "gay agenda." Call it whatever you like (protecting "traditional values," "family," "the sanctity of marriage"), there are three main battlefronts in the "war on gayety": gay marriage, gay parenting, and equal protection under the law.

Why Not Six Midgets and a Chicken?

The first and biggest of the three is gay marriage. If you have never heard the "Maha-Rushie" defend the ban, you're in for a real treat. I call it "Rush's Defense of Marriage Act," because it *has* to be an act.

Rush Defense #1: Marriage is a sacred institution not to be entered into lightly.

First, let's get the obvious out of the way. It's hard to take any comment seriously about the sanctity of marriage from a guy who's failed at it three times.

Second, if you're honestly concerned with protecting the sanctity of marriage, then you need to start by getting rid of no-fault divorce laws. No-fault divorce laws allow for the dissolution of a marriage for no reason other than because one party wants out. You don't have to prove abuse, or infidelity, or neglect, or anything—just say you want out, and you're out. Every state has no-fault divorce laws in one form or another with one exception: New York, a blue state. Not the state you were expecting? You were probably thinking Alabama, or Mississippi, or maybe Arkansas. However, divorce rates in the red states are 27 percent higher than divorce rates in the blue states, according to a 2003 study conducted by the National Center for Health Statistics.[1] So before you come down with a ban on gay marriage, you'd better lock down the sanctity of straight marriage first.

Rush Defense #2: Marriage has been between one man and one woman since time began.

True, yes . . . unless you look in the Old Testament, which is filled with polygamy. Back then, the world needed more children, so the practice of polygamy was accepted. Eventually it outlived its usefulness, so we moved on to monogamy. And while you could say we've been monogamous for a long time, thus making it the societal norm, if the Bible, which most dittoheads view as infallible, reflects a changing view on marriage and society concerning polygamy, shouldn't the same thing be true today concerning gay marriage?

Rush Defense #3: The purpose of marriage is to have kids, and gays can't reproduce.

Turns out, neither can Rush (he's childless in his three marriages), so that seems like an odd defense. Plus, I don't recall this being in the Bible, or the Constitution, or in any historical document that concerns marriage.

And that pretty well covers Rush's lines of defense.

But what about the hysterical slippery-slope defense of Rick Santorum, who says, "In every society, the definition of marriage has not ever to my knowledge included homosexuality. That's not to pick on homosexuality. It's not, you know, man on child, man on dog, or whatever the case may be. It is one thing. And when you destroy that you have a dramatic impact on the quality."[2]

First off, comparing gay marriage to bestiality is absurd— they have nothing to do with one another. A dog lacks the cognitive capacity to comprehend the concept of marriage. (Why you should have to explain this to another adult is mind-boggling, but for some reason you do.) Marriage is a legal contract, and as such it has to be entered into by two consenting adults who are legally able to represent themselves. A dog could no more enter a marriage than a chicken could sign a recording contract or a hamster could get a license to drive a car.

From the dittohead perspective, this issue is supposedly about protecting children and fighting back against the "secular left." But deep down (and I say this from personal experience), it is really about official condemnation of gay people in order to try and shame them back into the closet. Extending existing marriage laws to same-sex couples hurts no one, helps cut taxes (which Republicans *love*), and generates revenue for the states through licensing fees. Banning it shows that dittoheads don't view these relationships as legitimate.

Next Thing You Know They'll Be Adopting Children!

In the spring of 2005, the Tennessee legislature finally took on the "number one" issue facing our state. No, not TennCare, our "train flying off the rails" version of Medicare. Not being 46th in the U.S. in education. Not the huge budget shortfalls. Not the fact that our sales-tax system is crushing our state's poor. Not even that we're seeing our Homeland Security funding cut despite the fact that we have the busiest cargo airport in the world, or that we have over 2,000 children waiting for adoption.[3] Forget all of that. In the state House and Senate, legislature was pending to ban same-sex couples not from marriage . . . but from adopting children! This was the number-one issue in Tennessee—to stop gays from adopting children because . . . because why again?

The right's argument against gay marriage is that that they aren't discriminating against gay people, but protecting the sanctity of marriage. That argument may be wrongheaded and hypocritical, but at least it's an *attempt* at an argument. However, the argument for anti-adoption legislation seems to be "because we hate gays, we're enacting legislation to ensure that they are treated like second-class citizens, even though what they do isn't illegal."

As you know, it's been a long time since I was pro-life, but if memory serves, one of our less hateful slogans was "Adoption: A Loving Choice." The idea being that mothers should go ahead and have a baby, then give it up for adoption (and then regret that decision for the rest of their lives instead of regretting having an abortion for the rest of their lives). It's a fine principle, so why in the world would you pass laws restricting any group from being allowed to adopt a child? The answer that the right provides is as simple as it is wrong: They still believe that there's a link between homosexuality and pedophilia. Sure, there's no reputable scientific evidence to prove it, but remember, most dittoheads seem to believe that science denies God. As Stephen Colbert famously put it, most dittoheads have adopted the mentality of "You can keep your facts, I'm going with the truth!"

As I mentioned, Tennessee has over 2,000 wards awaiting adoption. Wards are great if you're a Batman looking to recruit Robins, but not so great if you have too many kids and not enough quality homes. If you're going to say that you really care about encouraging adoption, and thus preventing abortion, it seems like you might want to empty the state ward rolls first. Otherwise you're just advocating a position that's less "the loving choice" and more "Let the State Worry About It."

Sadly, dittoheads seem to have a natural instinct to promote policies that make the rate of abortions go up, while at the same time maintaining that they want fewer of them. Abstinence-only education does nothing to reduce the rate at which teenagers have sex, but it does significantly reduce the number of kids who wear a condom, which leads to unwanted pregnancies and situations like the one my friend Amy faced.

Furthermore, the number-two reason women give for having an abortion is that they were afraid they couldn't afford the financial responsibility of having a baby.[4] President Bush helps, of course, by making cuts to food stamps and Medicare. That's sure to help end abortion. And I suppose the prevailing wisdom of the anti-gay adoption movement is that more women will make "the loving choice" once they learn their kids won't be adopted by any of those "queers."

Daddy, What's a "Hate Crime"?

Rush likes to say that he opposes hate crime legislation because *all* violent crimes are hate crimes. I'll give him that. But what differentiates a "hate crime" from a "regular violent crime" (for lack of a better phrase) is the intended victim.

Let's say someone kills me in a mugging. He's got a gun, I put up a fight, the mugger shoots me dead. I'm really the only victim. Sure, my wife, family, and friends would be upset, but it was an act of random violence.

Now let's assume that I'm killed by a roving gang of youths for appearing to be gay. And after killing me, they string up my body from a bridge to intimidate other gay people. In this case, there's a clear message being sent: "If you're gay, you're next!"

Most dittoheads understand this. Ask them if they think there's a difference between collateral damage in Iraq and the stringing up of U.S. contractors from a bridge, and I think they'll see the point, unless they're completely unreachable. Hate crime legislation should apply to any crime in which the *intent* is to intimidate other members of the targeted group. When you understand the definition and the purpose of hate crime legislation, you can see how onerous opposition to it really is. By removing homosexuals explicitly from hate crime protection, you're implying that it's okay to kill this type of person, if it'll get the rest of them to shut up. I'm not saying that all crimes against homosexuals, or any minority for that matter, are hate crimes. What I'm saying is that everyone should have protection from crimes of intimidation. To accept anything less is just plain hateful.

The Sausage-Making Process Continues

I'm pretty sure at this point that any legislation that starts with the words "Gays aren't allowed to . . . " would pass overwhelmingly in Tennessee. My state is not alone. Legislation is pending in other states to exclude gay people from the protection afforded by hate crime legislation. Other states are trying to specifically exclude same-sex partners from sharing health benefits. The legislation is rapidly reaching a fever pitch. On the one hand, I find legislation like this so morally repugnant that I want to fight it with every fiber of my being. But the part of me that understands the "sausage making" process says to let the sexual McCarthyism continue. Maybe we should let the right beat the gray drumhead, so the average American can see their efforts for how disgusting it really are. It's hard to accept the idea that we have to let things get worse before they get better, but something's got to happen to change the zeitgeist.

It's very comfortable for dittoheads to say, "I don't hate gays,

I just want to see kids brought up in traditional homes," or "I don't hate gays, I just want to protect the sanctity of marriage." Don't let them get away with that. Instead, make them admit that they don't consider homosexuality normal, and that they want gay people to have diminished status in the eyes of the law. By making them face the truth, perhaps a few will realize the error of their ways, as I did. And, if we get a few of them to change their way of thinking, maybe we can carve out the 5 percent of Republican voters that we need to start winning elections.

17: THE RODNEY DANGERFIELD
OF ISSUES

•

A great cause for consternation among many in the progressive community is the inability of the environment to get any traction as an issue. It's frustrating, because if there's one issue that you think would be a priority, it's not screwing up the world we live in. But, like Rodney Dangerfield, the environment gets no respect.

Actually, there is a reason why people don't care about the environment. It's called an "availability bias." For example, most dittoheads hate gay people because they don't know any. They want to ban abortion because they've never known anyone who's had one. They want to cut welfare because they've never had to depend on it. If they have such myopia about issues whose painful, sometimes devastating effects are visible, how are we supposed to get them excited about what could happen 50 or a hundred years down the road? The problem with environmentalism is that it isn't tangible enough—you can't see it, you can't taste it, and most dittoheads feel like they can't even get a straight answer about it.

I was as guilty of this as anyone, as I never gave a flip about the environment for the vast majority of my life as a conservative. The "tangible" event for me was near the end of my dittiotism, when my father-in-law took me snowmobiling in Yellowstone National Park. If you've never gone snowmobiling in Yellowstone, I can tell you it's quite the study in contrasts. There you are in one of the most pristine and beautiful places in North America, riding the loudest, most foul-smelling contraption God ever allowed us to invent. Even after you're done, you can come back 30 minutes later and still smell the fumes. But aside from being a nuisance, I never really had much of an appreciation for how much damage those things were doing to the environment. Like I said, it was an "availability bias"—you don't think while you're riding, "I'm contributing 0.00000012 percent to the carbon dioxide problem."

The Population Bomb

I can't tell you how many times Rush used *The Population Bomb* as proof that global warming was a bunch of nonsense. *The Population Bomb* was a book written by Paul Ehrlich in 1968. In it, he made some fantastically horrific predictions (global famine, total exhaustion of resources, etc.), all of which failed to actually occur. Rush's logic was that because Paul Ehrlich's predictions didn't come true, global warming won't come true either. Given that Ehrlich wasn't even talking about global warming or climate change, I don't understand why this would be a convincing argument, but, as usual with Rush, it doesn't matter that it doesn't relate.

In 1994, the Environmental Defense Fund published *The Way Things Really Are: Debunking Rush Limbaugh on the Environment,* a report that was meant to "correct" the environmental statements that Rush had made on his show. Here are some of my favorite Rushisms from the report, along with the EDF "corrections": [1]

RUSH FICTION: "Algore's (That's what Rush called Al Gore—Algore, as in Igor to Clinton's Dracula) book is full of calculated disinformation. For instance, he claims that 98% of scientists believe global warming is taking place. However, a Gallup poll of scientists involved in global climate research shows that 53% do not believe that global warming has occurred, 30% say they don't know, and only 17% are devotees of this dubious theory."

SCIENTIFIC FACT: "These numbers, apparently from a George Will column of 3 September 1992, are supposed to show the findings of a Gallup poll taken in late 1991 to ascertain the opinions of research scientists concerning global warming. Nowhere in the actual poll results are there figures that resemble those cited by Will or Limbaugh. Instead, the poll found a substantial majority of the scientists polled, 66%, believed that human-induced global warming was already occurring. Only 10% disagreed, and the remainder were undecided."

RUSH FICTION: "A fact you never hear the environmentalist wacko crowd acknowledge is that 96% of the so-called 'greenhouse' gases are not created by man, but by nature."

SCIENTIFIC FACT: "The greenhouse effect is, by and large, a natural phenomenon, produced by gases in the atmosphere such as carbon dioxide (CO_2) and water vapor that have warmed the Earth for eons, enabling its climate to support life. However, in nature these gases usually remain in balance, leading to a stable climate, while the greenhouse gases added by humans over the last 200 years have accumulated to the point that the amount of CO_2 in the atmosphere, for example, is now more than 25% above what it had been for the previous 10,000 years. The scientific consensus is that the accumulation of CO_2 and other gases due to human activity will alter the climate substantially, warming the globe by three to eight degrees Fahrenheit over the next century."

I could go on. There are dozens of instances of Rush using pseudoscience, straw men, and lone voices of dissent as the basis for his attacks on the environment. He uses this technique on everything else as well, from evolution to nicotine addiction.

But rather than focus on the minutia of Rush's lack of scientific understanding, I'd rather talk about what I consider to be the funniest theory advanced by Rush, which is his belief that mankind couldn't destroy the Earth even if it tried. Rush's "hypothesis" is that if you buried all the world's nukes as deep in the earth as you could, then detonated them all at the same time, the resulting force wouldn't be anywhere near enough to blow the Earth into little tiny bits. I'm pretty sure his point is that the Earth is so powerful that it can adapt to whatever we humans throw at it. If we throw a bunch of pollution in the air, the Earth can handle it. In fact, if you think the Earth *can't* handle it . . . then you're no environmentalist. Let the Earth take personal responsibility for itself!

Following this logic to its natural conclusion, Rush and the dittohead nation at large believe the Earth will change to accommodate *us*. The Earth may indeed have a built-in balancing mechanism, but it doesn't necessarily follow that the mechanism will be one we approve of. Making too much carbon dioxide? The Earth can solve that—make more oceans! How do you do that? Raise the temperature a few degrees. Without realizing it, many dittoheads could very well be working against their own best interests (again).

The amazing thing is that the idea of global warming fits the dittohead understanding of the environment to a tee. It's the logical conclusion of how their thought process operates. The problem is pollution. Pollution is caused by people. To stop the pollution, a self-regulating Earth will act personally responsible and get rid of the source of the pollution (a.k.a. us). And yet dittoheads use this as justification for the opposite. This is because they subscribe to the theory of Intelligent Environmental Design. Once again we see a perspective whereby God and science are mutually exclusive. So if science says we're destroying ourselves, the answer must be that God will protect us! And since we're protected by divine providence, why worry about global warming?

The late, great comic writer turned environmentalist Douglas Adams once compared the mindset of those like Rush with that of a self-aware, intelligent puddle of water. When it becomes aware of its surroundings, the puddle notices how well it fits into every little nook and cranny of the hole it's in. After a while the puddle starts to think it's entirely too convenient that it fits its surroundings perfectly, and so it begins to think that the hole was designed for it. It's only logical. How else could it fit in so well? So as the sun rises, and the puddle starts to evaporate, it thinks, "I don't have anything to worry about. I was meant to be here. And who or whatever put me here in the first place will take care of me." Needless to say, it is something of a shock to the puddle when it completely evaporates in the afternoon sun.

Would You Like to Supersize Your Arsenic?

As I said, I understand why dittoheads don't get all worked up about the environment, but it rankles me that the issue can't even get traction among liberals and progressives. Again, I say this is an availability bias. Like evolution, most environmental changes are small and take a long time to develop. But I can tell you this for certain: Something's happening (and how many more hurricanes do we need to make the point?).

Even if we liberals and progressives can't passionately get behind the potential impact of global climate change, at a minimum we can stop the dittoheads from taking the issue away from us. Don't get me wrong. I don't really care who has ownership of this issue. If all of a sudden Bush proposed some real, meaningful environmental legislation, I'd be all for it. This isn't a red state problem or a blue state problem; it's *our* problem. We liberals need to see clearly on this issue, because the other side can't see through its own smog.

18 : THE WHOLE MADE-UP SOCIAL
SECURITY THING

•

Social Security is yet another example of the fundamental con-
flict between the Democratic and Republican worldviews. From
the Democratic perspective, Social Security is a perfect illustra-
tion of how the government can protect the most vulnerable by
providing a safety net for senior citizens. And if the idea was to
reduce poverty among people over the age of 65, then the program has been a resounding success! According to the Social
Security website, poverty among senior citizens has fallen from
29.5 percent as recently as 1967 to single digits today.[1] In fact,
in 2004 the poverty rate for seniors fell while the poverty rate
for the nation as a whole rose, according to the U.S. Census
Bureau.[2]

   But none of that is good enough for Rush. According to
him, all we've done with Social Security is to make a bunch of
otherwise capable senior citizens lazy. "Surely there must be a

way to apply the principles of Personal Responsibility to this nasty government entitlement program," Rush reasons. And so, after much brainstorming and think-tanking, in 2005 President Bush rolled out his plan to bring Social Darwinism to the masses—Social Security Private Accounts.

One of the arguments that conservatives like to use in favor of private accounts is that the current system is unfair. Under certain circumstances, they say, people can pay into Social Security for their entire lives and not receive any benefit. There are two reasons, however, why this isn't a particularly strong argument for private accounts.

The first involves the plan that Bush proposed, and its use of immediate annuities. A lot of people don't know what immediate annuities are, but they are important. When you buy an immediate annuity, you give up the rights to a large sum of money, and in return you get a guaranteed lifetime income. As an example, let's say you've got $500,000 that you want to live off of for the rest of your life. It would be easy to draw up a plan for that $500,000 if you knew the exact date you were going to die. But most of us don't have that luxury, so we go to an insurance company that says, "Sure, we'll take your $500,000 today, and give you $2,500 per month for as long as you live." This process is called "annuitizing," and it's irrevocable. You give up all rights to your original $500,000, but you now have the peace of mind that comes from knowing you'll never run out of money. That's the upside. The downside is, if you die tomorrow, there's nothing left to pass on to your heirs. Kind of like Social Security.

The President's plan didn't address this. Under his plan,

about half of the money you put into Social Security would be used to pay for a reduced version of the current system. The rest would go into your private account to invest as you see fit. So let's say you've reached retirement age, and you've got a private account worth $500,000. When you start collecting Social Security, half of your retirement income would be provided by the traditional system, and the other half would come out of the $500,000 in your private account.

Most people believe that you can take whatever amount you need out of your private account, and if you happen to die the day after you retire, you can just pass on whatever's left in your private account to whomever you see fit. But under the Bush plan, when you start drawing your traditional retirement benefit, you must purchase an immediate annuity with your private account. So if you die tomorrow, there's nothing left of your private account to pass on to your heirs . . . just like the current version of Social Security.

What we all have to remember (and to an even greater extent accept) is the idea that Social Security is an insurance program. People spend billions and billions of dollars every year on term insurance premiums, and over 90 percent of them never receive a dollar in benefits. But there isn't massive public outrage demanding the return of unused term insurance premiums, because most people instinctively understand the way insurance works—some people need it, some people don't, and the people who don't pay for the people who do. The system doesn't work when you give the money back to the people who don't need it.

Dittoheads agree with the president when he says that

Social Security is facing a cash-flow crisis and that by 2018 we'll be paying more money out of the system than taxpayers are paying into it. So his solution is to take money *out* of Social Security today to make it more solvent tomorrow. With that kind of logic, I'm starting to understand why Bush is running the United States as poorly as he ran any of his other businesses, from baseball to wildcatting. As with all things Bush, the principle sounds great, and the message is well packaged, but the execution is miserable. Bush policies tend to be all "Flash, Dash, and Cash." They're big on packaging, but short on substance.

Rush comes at the whole Social Security thing from an interesting angle, saying something along the lines of, "It was okay when Clinton proposed it, why isn't it okay now?" This may be the first time Rush has ever pointed to something Clinton did and said "See! That was a great idea!" What he fails to mention is that Clinton wanted to have the Social Security Trust Fund, and not individual investors, invest in things other than U.S. Treasuries with the surplus dollars that are raised by Social Security taxes, but not spent on benefits. "Oh," your dittiot coworker intones, "so it's okay for the government to invest in the market, but it's not okay for me to invest it?" Yes, that's absolutely what I'm saying.

To explain why, I'll have to go into my background a little. In my professional life I am a money manager, specifically a Certified Financial Planner. That's a fancy way of saying, "I tell people what to do with money, and I've gone to great lengths to ensure that I'm good at it." And in my seven-year career as a

CFP, I've come to one inescapable conclusion—the investment record of the "average investor" leaves much to be desired.

The Below-Average Performance of the Average Investor

The average investor buys at the top, and sells at the bottom. They lack patience, discipline, and the information necessary for good decision-making. They're reactionary, greedy, and easily frightened. Ask the average investor why they picked this fund over that fund, and the answer will be "because it did better last year." Never mind the fact that it was a tech fund, and tech funds were in vogue, and now the tech sector is overvalued, and the manager that actually got that return doesn't work for that fund anymore. "It did better, so it gets all my money."

Then the fund loses 50 percent, and the average investor gets nervous and sells at the bottom of the market. What will our average investor do now? Will he take the time to figure out how to create a balanced portfolio? No. He'll look and see what did well *last year* and invest in that. And so the cycle continues, with the average investor playing Tina to the market's Ike. "Don't worry, baby. The market's different now. It's not gonna hurt you."

Keep in mind, there is no shame in being an "average investor." In the eight years that led up to my becoming a financial advisor, I was one of the worst of the worst. But if I keep doing the same thing expecting different results (also known as insanity), shame on me. The larger problem with the president's plan is that no one is willing to cop to the fact that the average investor is less than capable when it comes to informed decision making.

Let's fast-forward 50 years to when the alleged Social Security crisis is supposed to come to a head. In 2056, Joe Investor has managed to set enough aside in his private account to buy an annuity that will pay him $17,000 per year. Those suckers who didn't take the private account option are only making $15,000 per year. But Joe Investor is invested entirely in a NASDAQ index fund (since it did great last year). Then the market does what the market does, which means over the next twelve months Joe's investment loses 50 percent of its value. "I've got to make that money back fast," Joe thinks. And so Joe begins the investment equivalent of playing the lottery, investing in penny stock after penny stock, hoping to hit it big. At the end of the day, Joe's left with the ability to purchase an annuity paying him only $11,000 per year (the $10,000 guaranteed benefit plus the paltry $1,000 annuity his remaining funds buy). Since Joe can't afford food AND medicine on such a stipend, he is now society's problem.

I'd like to say that this is a purely theoretical exercise, but it's already happened. My best year of getting new clients was 2003, when tons of baby boomers came to my office fearing they'd never be able to retire. And, sure enough, many of them had a portfolio of tech-heavy mutual funds that had lost 50 percent or more of their value. Fortunately they had Social Security to fall back on. But what if the problem was Social Security? What if during the two years leading up to your 65th birthday, it was 1999 all over again, and your self-directed Social Security Trust Fund lost 50 percent of its value? I think a lot of people would be saying, "Boy, it's too bad we don't have some kind of government program to secure society from such problems."

If you'd like to see some real outrage, just watch dittohead reaction to the idea that, by 2050, in order to keep from reducing benefits, we'll have to raise taxes by 4 percent! A 4 percent tax hike! Why . . . why . . . that'd wreck the economy! What about the children! What about the corporations! We'll have to fire people rather than pay 2 percent more in taxes (because you split your Social Security taxes with your employer). There'll be food lines! Unemployment will reach 50 percent! The streets will flow with the blood of the nonbelievers (which is going to happen anyway, but this will no doubt hasten it).

In reality, if you want to shore up Social Security, let the Trust Fund invest in things other than treasuries (via professional money managers who have a proven track record), and raise the employee-portion cap to $200,000. That generates more revenue to fund future obligations, and it keeps corporate lobbyists quiet by giving them some government money to play with. Best of all, it keeps the government from quietly wandering over and "borrowing" the Trust Fund money like they've done in every single year of the Bush administration. Think of it as being like an equity lock-box for future generations to enjoy.

Of All People, I Should Love This Plan

One of the worst signs for the president's plan is the fact that people like me hate it. I am, after all, in the investing business. You'd think I'd stand to rake in fat piles of cash if only Social Security had private accounts. Add to that the fact that I'm a white male living in a red state, and this proposal should be more of a slam dunk than WMDs in Iraq!

Conceptually, there's nothing untoward or evil about the concept of private investment in Social Security. And the idea of investing the Social Security Trust Fund in something other than treasuries isn't new. As I said, Clinton proposed taking some trust fund assets and investing them in commercial debt and equity instruments.

As is often the case, the devil is in the details. The "details" in this case lie in what type of private account an individual has. Will it be more like the government's Thrift Savings Plan, or will it be more like a private market IRA? For the small investor, which in this case means every taxpayer with a private account, the difference between the two is enormous.

For those unfamiliar with the government's Thrift Savings Plan, think of it as the world's largest 401(k). It gives three million federal employees (including members of Congress) access to private investment accounts for their retirement. Money is invested in one of five "sub-accounts." A sub-account is basically the same thing as a mutual fund, and each sub-account has its own investment strategy. An independent Federal Retirement Thrift Investment Board puts out bids for index funds to include in each plan. The sub-accounts cannot hold individual stocks or actively managed mutual funds. They can only hold index funds. Index funds are unmanaged (so the board can't pick a manager who buys only Halliburton stock, for example), and cheap (very low expense ratios).

The results have been impressive. Let's say you've got $2,000 you want to save for retirement, and you invest it in the Thrift Savings Plan. You want low risk, so you invest entirely in the G fund. These are Treasury Bonds that are backed by the full faith and credit of the U.S. Government, and as such are considered "no risk" investments. Had you invested your $2,000 on January 1, 2004, by December 31, 2004, your account would have been worth $2,086 after paying all applicable expenses. Remember that number—it'll come up again.

Now, let's assume the same scenario as above, but instead of investing in the TSP you decide to invest your $2,000 in an individual IRA at a major brokerage firm. I'll use my firm in this example, since I know the costs associated with our accounts. If you buy a "no-load" mutual fund, you'll pay a $40 transaction fee. So right off the bat you're 2 percent in the hole. My firm also charges $20 per quarter to maintain an account of that size, so you'll have to make at least 4 percent per year on whatever investment you choose just to break even.

Let's assume that you want to be safe, so you invest in U.S. Treasuries. We'll also assume that the current yield on a 30-year Treasury bond is 4.61 percent (which is what it was when I wrote this). Let's take a look at what happens to your intrepid little investment in its first year:

Initial Investment	$2,000.00
Less: Transaction Fee	$20.00
Plus: Interest Earned	$85.14
Less: Maintenance Fee	$80.00
Ending Balance	$1,985.14

You've just made the safest long-term investment available on the free market and you lost $15! And, as the broker on your account, I didn't make a dime. ("No-load" funds offer no compensation to the selling broker, hence the name "no-load.") Clearly I'm not going to be very motivated to give you much in the way of advice on this account.

Instead of using the working model of the Thrift Savings Plan, Bush's plan is to follow a more brokerage-like account strategy. But by using the Thrift Savings Plan as a model, the government would cut out the transaction and maintenance fees associated with most brokerage accounts. It's the first rule of the free market—the more people you have who want to buy, the less you should have to pay to get it. So why go with the private brokerage account model when we know it will end up costing the consumer more than it has to?

The reason is simple enough. Republicans don't think that free-market rules should apply to the government. They don't think the government should be able to buy prescription drugs directly, for example. And they don't want to use the successful TSP program as the model for Social Security's private accounts. Instead, they want to create a new program that effectively subsidizes private companies by creating 200 million new fee-based brokerage accounts. It's like they're saying, "Hey, this TSP thing is good enough for us . . . but you little people, you go do your own thing."

As is often the case with the Bush administration, everyone loses with this program. That's not terribly surprising when you take a look at their track record. We brought "democracy" to the Middle East, and oil prices are at an all-time high. Medicare has a prescription drug benefit now, and yet seniors are somehow paying more for prescription drugs then they were before the program was instituted. Social Security's no different. It faces a huge, long-term cash shortfall, so the answer is to borrow our way out of it?

Even though Bush's plan currently lies dormant, this is something that the Republicans will pick up again once the political climate is more favorable. Instead of creating a safety net, they want to create a net that's full of holes, which means a lot of people are going to fall through.

19: THE TAXES OF EVIL

•

You may have noticed that dittoheads really have a chip on their shoulders when it comes to taxes. Ever hear one complain about it? It goes something like, "I pay property tax, I pay sales tax, I pay state income taxes, I pay federal income taxes. I pay too much!" Ever wonder the reasons for their tax-related complaints?

Most dittoheads believe that the single largest category of government spending is on "entitlement programs" like welfare and unemployment insurance. "Entitlement programs" make it sound like there are things that people can't overcome on their own, thus denying the commandment of personal responsibility. And since no dittohead believes that there are obstacles that the individual shouldn't be able overcome on his own, they view spending on entitlement programs as not only wasteful, but as sacrilege. These programs, they argue, create a dependency class of unwilling workers suckling at the government teat. And since taxes fund these programs, dittoheads don't like to pay taxes.

There is also the belief that cutting taxes results in more federal revenue. "Reagan proved it," dittoheads argue, just like Reagan proved deficits don't matter. Actually, Reagan proved that America has great credit, a fact that the Republicans' current "tax-cut and spend" brand of big-government conservatism is about to change. But if cutting taxes led to more federal revenue, then we could reduce the federal tax rate to 0 percent and thus reap infinite tax rewards. Alternatively we could raise taxes to 100 percent and bankrupt the government. The absurdity of this doesn't matter to dittoheads, who still believe the dogma that tax cuts lead to increased economic activity, which, in turn, leads to more federal revenue.

As you can see, dittoheads have a dual frustration with taxes. They resent paying them, because their money will then be used to deny one of the central tenets of their political philosophy, personal responsibility. And they believe that by paying more in taxes, the government is actually making less money.

Peeing on the Poor: Trickle-Down Economics in Action

How did we get from lower taxes to increased economic activity? Through the process Bush 41 described as "Voodoo economics," which dittoheads call Trickle-Down Economics. The theory is that if you give money back to business owners in the form of lower taxes, they'll use that money to expand their businesses, which will lead to new jobs and the creation of new consumers/taxpayers.

However, businesses often use the extra money they receive from lower taxes to finance the moving of jobs overseas, or to purchase things that were made in other countries. That does, in fact, create new consumers/taxpayers, but, unfortunately, they usually live in the Philippines (or China, India, Vietnam, etc.), which is not very helpful to our economy.

And sometimes business owners just put the extra money back in their own pockets. I knew a dittohead small-business owner, and he and I would get into arguments after he found out I was a Born-Again Democrat. I tried not to be adversarial, because the harder you push, the harder they push back, but one day he just wasn't going to take no for an answer. After giving me the "I pay enough in taxes" line, I pointed out how, in my professional opinion, the Bush tax cuts should be allowed to sunset (which they're scheduled to do in 2011), and that we should go back to the tax rates we had in 2000.

He didn't want to hear this. "Raising taxes would ruin the economy!" he screamed. "Don't you understand? If taxes go up, I'd have to fire people. And I wouldn't be the only one. Business owners around the country would have to do the same!"

I asked if he was making money back in 2000. He said he was. So, I continued, it would stand to reason that whomever he could afford to employ in 2000 he could still afford to employ today. He agreed. I then asked if he had hired anyone since the Bush tax cuts were enacted. "No one," he said. If he hadn't hired anyone, I assumed his business was flat? Not so. He said that business had been great, and that the last two years had been his best ever.

At that moment, one of his employees came into the office, so I thought I'd have a little fun. I asked the employee how he had spent his raise from last year. "Hell, I haven't had a raise in over two years!" he responded.

Still, I gave the owner the benefit of the doubt. Maybe he'd spent his profits on expanding his business, or on some new equipment that would generate more revenue for the company? I asked him about this. Turns out the extra revenue had gone toward making payments on a new boat—that had been manufactured overseas! Yet he had been telling his employees that things were tight. Ah . . . trickle-down economics in action.

The National Sales Tax

One of the things Rush likes to go on about is how unfair the current tax system is. If you go to his website, you'll find a pie chart that shows how only the rich pay taxes.[1] He'll also link to supporting documentation showing that the top 50 percent of wage earners shoulder 95 percent-plus of the federal tax burden.

Like many things said by Rush, this is deliberately misleading. Excluded from his analysis are the taxes that are paid for Social Security and Medicare. That particular omission disproportionately eliminates those taxpayers earning $90,000 or less (i.e., most taxpayers) and makes it seem like the rest of us are just a bunch of freeloaders.

However, this misrepresentation is the springboard from which Rush jumps to the "fairest" method of taxation in his book— the National Sales Tax. Why should people pay different amounts in taxes when we could all pay the same, he asks? Forget deductible interest and marginal rates—Rush wants just one tax, on things you buy. Then, the more people buy, the more money the government makes. What a perfect system for the American zeitgeist!

On paper it seems like a great idea, and if poor people could eat paper then it would be wonderful! Unfortunately the poor have to eat things other than figurative pieces of paper, and sales taxes are particularly regressive when it comes to the basic needs of lower-income families. It's also punitive on fixed-income seniors, who represent a rather sizable and growing demographic in modern society.

To correct all this, why not try to make the National Sales Tax fairer by excluding certain things, say, medical expenses? Well, then all kinds of questions arise. Would hospital bills be taxed, for example? Those are some fairly large revenue-making transactions you're talking about giving up. Maybe we can get around the unfairness in an easier way, by exempting people below a certain income level? Well, then we're back to an income-based tax system. The point of all this is that once you start getting into "real life," the "fair and easy tax system" becomes less of both.

And this doesn't even address the ease with which consumers can avoid paying a National Sales Tax. While avoiding income tax involves complicated things like changing your citizenship or spending most of the year outside the country, avoiding a national sales tax involves nothing more difficult than buying stuff outside the country. That's as simple as changing your web bookmark from amazon.com to amazon.co.uk.

The Death of an Otherwise Good Tax

Nothing rankles dittoheads more than the Estate and Gift Tax, or "The Death Tax," as they like to call it. Rush views it as a way in which the government punishes achievers—by making them pay taxes from beyond the grave on stuff they've already paid taxes on when they were alive.

From 1977 through 2001, the Estate and Gift Tax system remained basically unchanged (under both Democratic and Republican administrations). In 2001, the Economic Growth and Tax Relief Reconciliation Act was passed, which has had the effect of making estate planning very difficult, as exclusions for estate and gift taxes—as well as the top marginal tax rates—are going to keep changing every year until the estate tax is eliminated in 2011.

Currently, if you leave everything to your spouse, you pay no estate taxes. (That's called the "Unlimited Marital Deduction.") The Estate Tax only comes into play when both spouses die and money and property are left to other family members. Even then there is a sizable exemption amount under which you don't owe any taxes, which has gone up each year since 2002; currently it's at $2 million. With a little bit of planning, an estate can pass its wealth from generation to generation with little to no difficulty.

Let me give you an example. Say you're $100,000 over the limit and want to avoid the estate tax altogether. You can take that hundred grand and move it into a charitable trust—say the American Heart Association. When you die, the American Heart Association gets the hundred grand, but while you're alive, you can live off the interest generated by that money. With the interest generated, the American Heart Association can take out a $100,000 life insurance policy on your life, with your family as the named beneficiary. So when you die, the charity gets your $100,000, your family gets the $100,000 from the life insurance policy (since you didn't own it, it's not included in your estate), and the federal government gets nothing. Here's the drawback— once you give that $100,000 to the charitable trust, you don't ever get it back. You've given it away!

This kind of thing has been done countless times by countless millionaires and billionaires. And that's the reason why so many wealthy people, such as Bill Gates and Warren Buffet, came out against the abolition of the estate tax a few years ago. At the time people fawned over how they were putting the public's benefit ahead of their own, but I suspect the real reason for their opposition was because Bill and Warren have already given away their figurative hundred grand, and if the law changed they would have given it away for no good reason. One of the greatest reasons for the superaffluent to make huge charitable donations will be rendered completely moot if the estate tax goes away.

In addition, today only 2 percent of estates are subject to the tax. But if the new system takes effect in 2011, anyone who owns stock and tries to pass it on to their kids will be affected—currently estimated at over 50 percent of Americans. So instead of having a completely avoidable tax that affects only 2 percent of Americans, we'll have an unavoidable tax that will affect over 50 percent of the population! And yet many middle-class families are clamoring for this tax to be repealed. Suffice it to say that the repealed estate tax will do the same thing that most Republican doctrine does: shift the tax burden from those who *can* afford to pay to those who *can't*.

And that seems to be the bottom line for dittoheads. From their perspective, the poor have been drifting along with no incentive to contribute to society, and they have been left footing the bill. Shifting the tax burden from the top taxpayers to those at the bottom gives dittoheads the ability to say, "Look, poor people! This is what it's like to pay taxes! So quit living off our largesse!"

What they don't realize is that while they think they're thumbing their noses at the poor, they're actually cutting it off to spite their face. The entire dittohead nation can't possibly be in the top 2 percent of estates, or even the top 50 percent of income earners. Many, if not most, are just regular, working-class folks. If Rush has his way, instead of subsidizing programs that help the less fortunate, we'll all be underwriting the Chief Dittohead's new tax-free lifestyle.

Sometimes you just have to stand back and marvel at how good Rush is at convincing people to act counter to their own best interests! It's like an Orwellian wet dream:

WAR IS PEACE! FREEDOM IS SLAVERY! IGNORANCE IS STRENGTH!

20 : DITTOHEAD JUDICIAL PHILOSOPHY— CONSISTENTLY INCONSISTENT

•

Many folks know that a fortune cookie fortune is often made funny by adding the words "in bed" to the end of it. For example: "A pleasant surprise is in store for you" becomes "A pleasant surprise is in store for you in bed." So it is with dittohead judicial philosophy, except you change "in bed" to "on abortion."

During my life as a dittohead (pre-Amy), I towed the party line when it came to conservative judicial philosophy, which meant supporting judges who would vote to overturn *Roe v. Wade*. But since a plurality of Americans believe in keeping *Roe* legal, the Republicans couldn't come right out and say, "We're going to overturn *Roe v. Wade*." So words had to be invented to cloak that position in a more nebulous shroud. Thus the terms "activist judges" and "states' rights" were born. In addition, the anti-abortion position could be wrapped in the flag in the form of "strict constructionist," raising the question, "Who would the founding fathers abort?"

"Republicans Don't Want Activist Judges . . ."

By definition, the term "judicial activism" seems to indicate a predilection toward overturning established laws. Congress says, "you can't do x," and along comes some "activist judge" to throw the law out and say, "Oh yes you *can* do x! To say otherwise is unconstitutional!" This is why Republicans supposedly are against what they call "activist judges."

If that's the definition, however, then that's bad news for dittoheads. A July 6, 2005, op-ed piece in the *New York Times* looked at the judicial records of the then current Supreme Court justices.[1] They found that the most "activist judge" on the court was Clarence Thomas, who called congressional law unconstitutional over 65 percent of the time. Antonin Scalia was third at just over 56 percent. The judges who voted least frequently to invalidate congressional law? Stevens, Ginsberg, and Breyer—widely cited by dittoheads as the poster children of activist judges.

How can this be? Because the dittohead definition of an activist judge is actually "pro-choice liberal." And to a large degree, the only type of "judicial activism" the right cares about is that which concerns *Roe v. Wade.* With the stroke of a pen, dittoheads argue, activist judges took the right to decide abortion away from the people and invented a constitutional right. Rush calls this type of behavior "legislating from the bench," but it's not. The civil rights movement, for example, was about applying existing laws to African-Americans who had previously been excluded; the gay marriage debate is much the same. We're not talking here about creating new laws out of judicial decisions— we're just talking about to whom the law applies and to whom it doesn't.

"We Want Judges Who Believe in States' Rights . . . "

In addition to not wanting activist judges, Republicans also say they want judges who believe in "states' rights." "States' rights" is the dittohead foil to the "constitutional right to privacy" argument of the pro-choice movement. Dittoheads argue that state law should decide the abortion issue, and that the federal government should just stay out of it.

I wouldn't object to the dittoheads' belief in "states' rights" if it were consistent. The problem is, it isn't. Do dittoheads believe that "states' rights" should apply to gay marriage? Based on the rationale for the Federal Marriage Amendment's banning same-sex marriage, the answer seems to be no. What about the War on Drugs? Is it okay for Oregon to allow marijuana smoking? Based on Rush's objection to medicinal marijuana laws, that answer appears to be no as well. When dittoheads can't get the laws they want passed locally, like banning gay marriage and medical marijuana, they try to override them with federal law. With issues like abortion, they want the opposite. There's nothing inherently wrong with wanting to further your own agenda. Just don't try to pretend that it's based on some sort of unwavering belief in "states' rights," because it isn't.

" . . . and Who Are Strict Constructionists."

By definition, a strict constructionist is a judge who will "literally" interpret the Constitution (just like he might "literally" interpret the Bible). If it ain't "literally" defined in the Constitution, then the federal government has no right to do it. It is the final and ultimate truth as revealed to the founding fathers by God Himself.

A strict constructionist isn't going to agree with the idea of a "constitutional right to privacy," because those exact words don't appear in the Constitution (just like the words "separation of church and state" don't). But the term hasn't always meant that. President Nixon first used "strict constructionist" to describe justices who wanted stop the expansion of the rights of criminal defendants. In the 1970s, the term was applied to affirmative action. It was only in the 1980s that it began to apply more to social issues. Which leads us to today, when it has basically become code meaning "judges who would overturn *Roe*." How ironic that a term that is meant to describe a concrete and timeless understanding of the Constitution has itself been quite malleable over the last 30 years.

The problem with the strict constructionist philosophy is that, other than Nostradamus, there are few people who feel they can clearly define and illustrate how issues should be decided 200 years in the future. If we're talking original intent, the founding fathers originally intended only wealthy, white, male landowners to vote, and thought that treating people as property was okay. Somewhere along the way our stance on those issues seems to have changed. The founding fathers didn't plan for abortion or gay marriage in much the same way as we haven't planned for the legal rights of artificial intelligence. Realizing they could never address all issues throughout the whole of time, the founding fathers didn't leave us with a fixed and unwavering document. They left us instead with the next best thing—a flexible document that we could change to meet the needs of the day. The founding fathers didn't consider the Constitution as a holy document, and neither should we. It's possible to have a respect for history without becoming a slave to it.

If "activist judges," "states' rights" and "strict constructionists" were unwavering, unchanging principles, dittoheads would have to condemn Thomas and Scalia and accept gay marriage in states in which it was made legal. Since that's not likely to happen, all I can say is, these supposed unwavering core principles don't seem all that unwavering. What was once a simple set of legal principles has become, "We want nonactivist judges (unless they're conservative) who will give states' rights priority (unless it's on an issue that the states decide wrong, according to us), and we want a strict constructionist who will make rulings like he's a cast member from Colonial Williamsburg." All three terms are just an attempt to obfuscate something that would be unpopular if it were stated plainly. And if you have to obfuscate your core principles, maybe you don't have core principles in the first place.

21 : WHY TORTURE MATTERS

•

I was outraged by Abu Ghraib because it fit the profile of America that Al Qaeda was trying to portray in their propaganda. If we had been actually trying to make a recruitment video for the terrorists, we couldn't have done a better job. The Abu Ghraib scandal was a time for the nation to come together and say, "This is not what we stand for. The people who perpetrated these acts will be punished." Instead, this is what we got from Rush:

> "[What happened at Abu Ghraib] is no different than what happens at the Skull and Bones initiation and we're going to ruin people's lives over it and we're going to hamper our military effort, and then we are going to really hammer them because they had a good time. You know, these people are being fired at every day. I'm talk-

ing about people having a good time, these people, you
ever heard of emotional release? You ever heard of the
need to blow some steam off?" (*The Rush Limbaugh
Radio Show*, May 4, 2004)

If the photos outraged those in the Muslim world, comments like Rush's gave Al Qaeda dust-jacket material. I had
hoped at the time that some of the religious elements of Rush's
audience would rise up and say, "No! You can't do this in my
name!" However, the same people who watched two hours of
Jesus being tortured in Mel Gibson's movie looked at the Abu
Ghraib photos and said, "Eh, that's not so bad." Instead of drawing a line between appropriate interrogation techniques and outright torture, dittoheads went with the tactic of saying that both
were okay.

The most mind-boggling dismissal of the accusations of
abuse came from U.S. Representative Duncan Hunter of California, who used the menu being served to detainees as evidence
that no funny business was going on. Standing next to a plate of
chicken, rice, and two kinds of fruit, Hunter stated, "The
inmates in Guantanamo have never eaten better, they've never
been treated better. . . . The idea that we are somehow torturing
people in Guantanamo is absolutely not true, unless you consider
eating chicken three days a week is torture."[1] Instead of having a
dialogue on right and wrong and the soul of our nation, we were
being told that what we're doing couldn't be wrong because the
detainees were well fed?

Regardless of whether you're a dittohead or a Democrat, torture should bother you. We absolutely must be sure that in fight-

ing our enemies we haven't *become* our enemies. I'd also like to know that our elected representatives understand the difference between a menu and morality.

Are You Ignorant, or Just a Bad Person?

To find some common ground here, let's first dismiss what the actual detainees have been saying about being tortured. They have a reason to lie, dittoheads will say, whether they do or not. Also let's forget about information provided by the Red Cross, the U.N. or Amnesty International, as it's easy for dittoheads to tune out when they hear information from those sources.

Instead, let's only use information from the right-wing media, or information that is released directly by the government agencies responsible for oversight via Freedom of Information Act (FOIA) requests. If it was released because of FOIA, it's because someone didn't want you to see it, and I take such information to be accurate and unbiased. I also place a premium on what CIA and FBI agents who have visited the detention center have to say.

How Many of the Detainees at Gitmo Did Nothing Wrong? We Won't Know If We Don't Charge Them!

In May of 2004, the U.S. government released four British citizens who had been held for two years at Guantanamo Bay. Upon returning to England, Scotland Yard held them for a few days and then released them without charge. In short, they had done nothing wrong. In addition, according to Fox News, as of August 22, 2005, there were 505 people in custody at Gitmo whom we had yet to charge with a crime.[2] This kind of sounds like something the founding fathers would have frowned upon, as the Fifth Amendment makes clear:

"No person shall be held to answer for a capital, or otherwise infamous crime . . . nor be deprived of life, liberty, or property, without due process of law . . . "

I believe, and the founding fathers seem to agree, that if you're going to detain someone, you should really get around to charging them with *something*, be it terrorism, murder, conspiracy, bribery, extortion, tax evasion, whatever.

However, if you say this to dittoheads, they will go off half-cocked, saying that you want to turn the war against Al Qaeda into a "police investigation," like Clinton did. This is an old dittohead trick, to "Clintonize" the debate. Dittoheads look at Clinton's approach to fighting the war on terrorism like it was a police action rather than a military action. And that's true. Clinton was more interested in stopping people here than he was in putting boots on the ground over there. But that's because he was living in a pre-9/11 world. And, as I've said before, if you're going to say everything changed after 9/11, then you have to accept the fact that everything was different before it as well. Reagan and Bush 41 used the exact same strategy to combat terrorism (from Beirut to Pan Am flight 103), so if Clinton's guilty of anything, it's being just like his predecessors. But this argument won't resonate with dittoheads, because their idea is to make any non-Republican approach sound like something Clinton would do. If they can make something sound Clintony, then the dittohead mind can dismiss it immediately without having to consider the reason of the argument.

But even if we were talking about conducting the so-called "War on Terror" as a police investigation, consider this: From an historical perspective, the Nuremburg Tribunal was a "police investigation," and it seemed quite capable of dispensing justice in a quick and efficient manner. A procedure was followed, and justice was served. When you're taking potentially innocent people captive, I think it's imperative to follow some sort of procedure to make sure justice is done. Based on the wording of the Fifth Amendment, the founding fathers agree.

But forget about the founding fathers and police investigations and the "everything's different after 9/11" rhetoric. How about we just play by the rules because we're the good guys? A simple, moral argument that may sway some dittoheads.

What Torture Techniques Would Jesus Have Used?

In December of 2004, the ACLU received the email records of an FBI agent who was investigating allegations of torture at Gitmo. The agent described horrific things such as "strangulation, beatings, [and] placement of lit cigarettes into the detainees' ear openings . . . "[3] This didn't come from Amnesty International, or the Red Cross, or even former detainees. An actual FBI agent went to Gitmo and came back and told us what he saw. Not only that, but he also complained that there appeared to be an effort to cover up what was going on.[4] Here's a thought—if you're so ashamed of what you're doing that you have to cover it up, maybe you shouldn't have done it in the first place.

People are being tortured at Abu Ghraib and Guantanamo Bay. We're spitting in the faces of the founding fathers by doing this. And we're spitting on Jesus by calling the torture techniques that were used on Him acceptable if we do it to the "right" people. If you can honestly look at all of this and say, "Yeah, none of this bugs me," then we don't have anything more to talk about. And sometimes, that is sadly the case, and you have to accept the fact that you can't always talk to a dittohead. But honestly, I don't see how anyone can say that none of this bothers them and still claim to be a good Christian and a good American. And that is what you should tell a dittohead, whether or not they listen to you.

22: THEY ARE THE PARTY OF THE MILITARY. WE ARE THE PARTY OF THE TROOPS.

•

Republicans poll very high as being the "party of the military." And truth be told, they do love the actual nuts-and-bolts of the military: "Need a new artillery system to fight off the Russians, even though they're not the enemy anymore? You got it!" "Looking for a missile shield that only works if the enemy is kind enough to slap a homing device on their warhead? Sold!" "Want tactical nuclear weapons to blow up dictators in bunkers, regardless of civilian casualties? Who do I make the check out to?" Rush describes the primary role of the military as "killing people and breaking things," and when it comes to those activities in the abstract, dittoheads are all for them.

But the actual people who do the killing and the breaking? That's where "compassionate conservatism" seems to break down. When I was still a dittohead, during the early days of the current war with Iraq, I espoused notions like "Hey, they volunteered." Or, "As long as casualties in Iraq are less than Vietnam I think things are going well." I even put a "Support Our Troops" magnet on my SUV!

However, when Democrats asked if we could give the troops some armor, dittoheads like me took the Rumsfeld line and responded, "Well, you can have all the armor in the world and still get blown up." And since our troops weren't protected by adequate armor, an inordinate number of them were—and are—getting wounded. But when Democrats asked if we could have some money for veterans' health care, dittoheads responded, "Well . . . I'm not sure where we'd get that from. We're kind of strapped for cash at the moment."

Democrats, not Republicans, are the ones who want those who serve to have the maximum protection from hostile forces. Democrats, not Republicans, are the ones who want to provide veterans with health care. Democrats, not Republicans, are the ones who want to know that the president has a clear plan for winning the Iraq war. As Bush himself said during Kosovo, "Victory Means Exit Strategy."[1] If you're going to win a war, you have to define victory. To say that "it's done when it's done" is unacceptable, and it dishonors our men and women in uniform. Yet when Democrats question this strategy, they are called unpatriotic.

It's frustrating for Democrats to know all of this and still hear about how the Republican Party is the party of the military. How can Democrats get their message across against a perspective that has been historically skewed toward Republicans? One simple sentence:

They are the party of the military; we are the party of the troops.

Liars! Cowards! War Heroes?

Have you ever seen one party run so consistently and so negatively against those who actually served in the military than the current Republican Party? Think about what the Republicans say whenever the Democrats run a candidate who served in the military:

"Max Cleland? Liar and a coward. Blew himself up when he was drunk with a grenade, then tried to act like he was being all heroic."

"John Kerry? Liar and a coward. Shot himself in the ass and lied about it to get medals."

"Paul Hackett? Liar and a coward. Never saw actual combat! He's trying to make himself out as a war hero, but he's just a desk jockey!"

They even went after one of their own in the same way, when Bush attacked former POW John McCain during the 2000 Republican primaries.

How one can use the words "liar and coward" in *support* of a Republican politician, particularly George W. Bush, seems mysterious to Democrats. However, one mistake I think Democrats make is to settle for the excuse that "Republicans do it because they're evil." That kind of thinking is as functionally flawed as saying that terrorists want to kill us because "they hate our freedom." There is, at its core, a rationalization for the Republican party's anti-troop behavior. And to defeat the enemy you must first understand them.

Vietnam Syndrome

The Vietnam War was such a formative process in the shaping of the dittohead worldview that they see all opposition to Iraq through the lens of their Vietnam experience. That's why they get so bent out of shape when they talk about today's anti-war movement. Any time they see a war protester, they see Jane Fonda manning the VC anti-aircraft guns. They see Cindy Sheehan calling the troops baby killers.

The core constituency of this "troop hating" wing of the Republican Party comes from the Vietnam-era Nixon Republicans. These were the people who used every means necessary to avoid service in Vietnam—college deferrals, making babies, whatever it took to avoid going "over there." As Dick Cheney so famously put it, he had "other priorities" than fighting in the war. In that way, I think they are no different from the war protesters, as both groups, for different reasons, didn't think the Vietnam War was worth dying for.

But Nixon-era dittoheads don't share this belief. They see themselves as being the antithesis of the war-protest movement. They feel that their support for the broad concept of a "War on Communism" was enough, and that they didn't have to actually fight in the war. Today, these are the people who have a "Support Our Troops" magnet on the back of their Excursion, but when the VA asks for more funding, they respond by saying they don't want to "throw money at the problem."

This has created the disconnect that the average war-dodging dittohead embodies today. While they support the war, their actions suggest that they don't care about the people who actually fight it. I've thought of three possible motivations for this behavior:

1) Regret—Many dittoheads feel that they wasted an opportunity during the 1960s. Not an opportunity to fight, mind you, but an opportunity to party. Say what you will about hippie culture, but it sure looked like a whole hell of a lot of fun. Many of the "other priority" Republicans have only had sex with one person (their wife), never did drugs, and have all of the pressure of adulthood (work, kids, etc.) without having blown off any steam (pardon the pun) during their college years. One middle-aged dittohead friend of mine once admitted that he regretted having never tried marijuana in the '60s. I think many dittoheads regret having missed out on all the fun of the counterculture, even if they hated the politics. Somewhere in the cockles of their hearts, they wished they had been hippies.

2) Guilt—Many Republicans no doubt feel some form of "survivor's guilt" over having avoided serving in Vietnam. In a perverse sort of way this guilt manifests itself as a form of jealousy toward those who actually did serve.

3) Absolution—Deep down, many Republicans know that what they did during Vietnam was wrong. For every one of them who got a deferral, there's one who didn't. And whether that one who didn't made it out or not, his life was forever changed by the experience. How do you deal with the knowledge that your actions may have ruined or even ended someone else's life?

It's difficult for dittoheads to mesh their current gung-ho attitudes with their cowardly actions in the past. The way they handle it is to create a way for someone to have served their country, yet still remain a coward. It is vital for the dittohead mind to find those who *did* serve to have been just as cowardly as those who *didn't*. Only then will they find closure.

This is what they did with Paul Hackett. In their minds, if they could impugn the motives for his service, then the service itself would become meaningless. So they tried to imply that he was just a "desk jockey" or a "paper pusher," and that he served in some cushy post while in Iraq. For the record, is there any cushy posting in Iraq? I know this much—it sure as hell isn't in Fallujah, which is where Hackett served.

Then there's the Max Cleland approach. Max is a decorated Vietnam veteran and a triple amputee. "Wow . . . how do you get a guy like that?" the dittohead mind thinks. Maybe you could imply that his injuries were the result of a drunken prank, and that they occurred far from combat. You follow that by implying that he lied about how he got his injuries in order to make political hay. Bingo! He's a liar and a coward, and therefore he doesn't have to be respected!

John Kerry, of course, got the double whammy, as the right pulls out all the stops for presidential elections. To disrespect Kerry, the dittohead mind first accepted as gospel the idea that he only enlisted because he knew he'd run for president someday. Then, once he was in Vietnam, he shot himself repeatedly to get the three Purple Hearts he needed to get back home. The two Bronze Stars? All he did was run down an unarmed kid for the first one and make up an after-action report for the second.

Everyone knows this, even if every piece of evidence proves the opposite, and the only thing supporting the idea is the recently changed eyewitness accounts of people who disagree with him politically. (Oh, and never mind the fact that some of these eyewitnesses profited from business relations with the current administration.) Those facts are a buzz kill. We need to be able to believe that Kerry was just as much of a wimp as we were during Vietnam.

We often talk about how the right likes to create equivalencies between unlike political realities. So well rehearsed in this practice are they that they even use it to rationalize their own subconscious emotions. "I didn't serve," they think, "but the troops who did are no better than me!" This rationalization goes beyond simple denial or cognitive dissonance—it's about trying to get the yellow monkey of cowardice off of their collective college-deferred 4F backs.

23 : THE LOG IN RUSH LIMBAUGH'S EYE

•

You may have noticed that dittoheads are capable of incredible feats of mental gymnastics when it comes to defending Rush's beliefs. That's why you won't score a whole lot of points with them by saying, "Rush is wrong!" But where you can potentially have some success cracking their worldview is through pointing out places where Rush uses double standards or is intellectually dishonest.

I'll Define You, But You Can't Define Me!

If you've ever spent time listening to Rush, you know that one of his favorite things is to play a clip of some prominent Democrat saying something reasonable, and then stop the tape to insert his own commentary of "what it really means." It's a way for him to use bogus source material to misrepresent someone else's point of view.

Take torture. As you know, Rush downplayed the Abu Ghraib photos, comparing them to a fraternity prank, just folks "blowing off some steam." By itself this is a reprehensible position, but Rush took it a step further by using it to define his opposition.

As part of his rant, Rush described the photos as being "pictures of homoeroticism that looks like standard, good old American pornography."[1] In reaction to this, a prominent Democrat, Senator Tom Harkin, asked on the Senate floor if Rush's statement represented the view of the average American. Here is how Rush "commented" on Senator Harkin's response:

LIMBAUGH: Let's go to the audio tapes. We're going to start with the Harkin floor debate on me and this program. . . . This is a portion of his remarks. They're debating the defense authorization bill, but Harkin is upset that I dominate so much of Armed Forces Radio Network and that so few progressives have a chance to be heard. . . . He goes back to the Abu Ghraib quotes now to, in order—now, remember, what he's tryin' to do is get a bunch of liberal hosts that you can't listen to and you've never heard of on Armed Forces Radio Network. So in order to do that—he can't build them up—he has to try to tear me down.

HARKIN [audio clip]: Here's what Rush Limbaugh had to say about Abu Ghraib. He called it "a fraternity prank."

LIMBAUGH: Yes.

HARKIN [audio clip]: He dubbed the humiliation of inmates "a brilliant maneuver, no different than what happens at the Skull and Bones initiation at Yale."

LIMBAUGH: Stop the tape a second. Now, this, this is classic because he is taking this out of context, which is proof that they don't get the joke. Skull and Bones, that's John Kerry, that's George Bush. These guys—and there are all kinds of secret things that go on at Skull and Bones, and it was a laugh line. And here is this guy, outraged and taking it seriously. Not getting it—probably on purpose—but I doubt that he would have gotten it if he'd have heard it in context originally.

HARKIN [audio clip]: He described the images of torture as—again, a quote from Rush Limbaugh—"pictures of homoeroticism that look like standard, good old American pornography."

LIMBAUGH: Stop the tape! Yes, he's quoting me accurately, and I said, "Why are people upset about this when they buy it on cable TV, they buy it on the Internet, and they buy it in magazines every week? I thought we were supposed to love homoerotic things. I thought we were supposed to be open-minded and tolerant to homoerotic things. I thought that was the definition of an open mind, a large mind." So here I say, "Hey, there are a lot of people look[ing] at these pictures probably gettin' turned on." This is good! They are lookin' at these pictures and they're thinking, "America is advancing. Now the military's getting into it." Over their heads! Flat, smack-dab over their heads! Let's listen to the rest.

HARKIN [audio clip]: That's Rush Limbaugh talking to our troops 100 percent of the time. He said of the pictures at Abu Ghraib—and, again, this is quote from Rush Limbaugh—'If you take these pictures and bring them back and have them taken in an American city and put on an American website, they might win a video award for the pornography industry.' I ask, does this represent the views and attitudes of the average American citizen?

LIMBAUGH: No, no, of course not. But it does represent the views of the average American leftist! It's the left that will not condemn any of this when it happens to their kids, when it's happening in schools, when it's happening in the porno industry in this country. . . . Senator Harkin, your crowd is the one that's totally tolerant of this, except when it happens in a prison to our enemies![2]

Did you notice the way Rush used the sexually demeaning nature of the Abu Ghraib photos to define "leftists" as more or less sexual deviants? The premise is false, and the conclusion is false, but in Rush's world that is okay, because even though the material the opinion is based upon is bogus, according to Rush it represents an accurate summation of someone else's—in this case Harkin's—point of view.

Memogate, Anyone?

Based on his reaction to the Harkin comments, you'd think that Rush would be okay with other stories where, while the source material was false, the overall conclusion was still an accurate representation of someone else's point of view. Well, not quite.

Remember, prior to the 2004 election, when CBS aired the story regarding Bush's service (or, rather, lack thereof) in the Air National Guard? The memos that formed the basis of the story supposedly showed what everyone in the world already knew— that Bush had a spotty attendance record in the Alabama National Guard but was never called up to active duty (the usual punishment for such dereliction of duty), likely for political reasons (a.k.a. his father's influence).

Bob Mintz, who served in the 187th Air National Guard in Montgomery, Alabama, at the time that Bush was supposedly there, lives about a half mile from me. You may remember him from the Texans for Truth ad that ran during the 2004 campaign. The ad was basically a parody of the Swift Boat Veterans for Truth ads. In it, Mintz said that when he heard President Bush say he served with the 187th, he thought, "Really? I don't remember seeing him there." It turned out that out no one remembered seeing Bush in Montgomery.

"Memogate" revolved around a series of memos that supposedly revealed that Bush's commander, Lt. Col. Jerry Killian, ordered that Bush be suspended from flying for failure to perform his duties. One memo detailed how Killian was under pressure from his superiors to "sugar coat" Bush's flight evaluations.

When I first heard the story, my reaction was "and?" We knew all this stuff already. Bush had a six-month gap in his pay that he could never really explain. But that didn't matter to the right-wing blogosphere. When they heard the story, they acted as though Dan Rather were the devil incarnate, and started putting out reports that the memos were fake. The main basis for their claims was that typewriters didn't exist back in the early 1970s that could do superscripting. As a result, they alleged that the memos could only have been written in Microsoft Word. Suddenly the news media had need for the most specialized (and otherwise useless) people in all of journalism—font experts.

Accusations flew that the memos were fake! And, there was only one person we could turn to for answers. No, not Killian— he's dead—but Killian's former secretary, Marion Knox. Here's what Knox had to say in her own words, as reported to the Drudge Report:

"I typed memos that had this information in them, but I did not type these memos. There are terms in these memos that are not Guard terms but that are Army terms. They use the word 'Billets.' I think they were using that to refer to the slot. That would be a non-flying slot the way we would use it. And the style . . . they are sloppy looking." [3]

Despite this, Knox stood by the accusations contained in the allegedly fraudulent documents, that Bush skirted a medical and flight exam without suffering institutional repercussions.

"The information in these memos is correct—like Killian's dealing with the problems . . .

"It was General Staudt . . . that was putting on the pressure to whitewash Bush. For instance he didn't take his flight examination or his physical. And the pilots had to take them by their birthdays. Once in a while there would be a reason why a pilot would miss these things because some of them were commercial pilots. But they had to make arrangements to take their exams."

Some conservatives speculated that Ms. Knox was lying because she didn't like Bush. If that were so, why wouldn't she just lie about writing the memos? Why tell half a lie? In short, the basis of this story is false, but the material contained in the story is factually accurate. So Rush gave this story a pass, right? Well . . .

Here is Rush "commenting" on a clip from *Hannity and Colmes*.[4]

RUSH: Marcia Kramer, the reporter, interviewed Dan Rather and she said, "Do you still think that the documents are authentic?"

RATHER: The story is true. . . . If it turns out that they [the memos] are not authentic, I believe they are, but if it turns out they aren't, I'd like to break that story.

RUSH: Earth to Dan! [Laughing.] What can you do

but laugh? The story was "broken" a week ago today, Dan.

Rush thought the story was "broken" because the evidence it was based on *may* have been fabricated. When he goes back to the clip Alan Colmes asks this question of Col. Killian's son Gary:

COLMES: Marian Carr Knox, your father's secretary, says she thinks the documents are fake, but that they accurately reflect your father's point of view.

Now, Rush has heard that the potentially fabricated memos may still accurately portray the point of view of Bush's commanding officer. As the final arbiter of right and wrong for the whole dittohead nation, surely Rush would accept that there may be some validity to the story, right? Not so! Why then does Rush believe this story to be invalid?

RUSH: Sources remain questionable.

And so . . .

RUSH: This is not classic journalism. Well, you know, I say it's not "classic journalism," but is it what classic journalism has become? It is agenda-driven journalism, as practiced by CBS, and they've been caught. They've been caught red-handed, and really you can't illustrate it any better than to say this is Nixonian.

Looks like Rush got caught red-handed, too. Questionable sources invalidate the Memogate story, but false pretenses didn't invalidate his "Democrats are perverts" analogy. This sounds like "agenda-driven" journalism to me. It seems that in Rushworld, Republicans are free to quote the straw man effigies they create of Democrats, but Democrats should never rely on information that could in any way be challenged. In fact, Democrats should consider reporting to relocation camps now to avoid the unpleasantness of house-to-house searches later on. And that, my friends . . . is a direct quote!

24 : TREPPENWITZ

•

You know those moments in life when, a couple of hours after something happens, you think of what you wished you had said instead of what you actually did say? In German, that phenomenon is called "Treppenwitz," which literally means "the wisdom of the stairs." In my life, it's called "the day I met Al Franken."

In April 2005, Al brought his radio show to Memphis to do a live broadcast from the National Civil Rights Museum. A week earlier, I had stood in line at a car dealership to get tickets. I was the 71st person in line. They stopped giving tickets out at 75. Needless to say I was thrilled.

Before the show, the local Air America affiliate was hosting a "Breakfast with Al Franken/Autograph Session." I was finally going to have the opportunity to thank Al in person for helping to cure my dittiot-itis!

The day of the show I got up at a ridiculous hour to wait in line to have breakfast with Al. However, many of my progressive brethren got there even earlier than I did. As the morning wore on and I was still standing in the same place as when I arrived, I became concerned that I was going to miss Al.

Just when I was about to give up and go home, the line started moving. I went inside . . . and there was Al, sitting at a table, a signature Southern breakfast of eggs, bacon, grits, and a side of grease before him. As I got closer and closer, my nerves got worse and worse. I don't get star-struck very often, but this was one of those times.

Then I was before him.

"Um . . . Mr. Franken?" I stammered, holding my copy of Al's book *Oh, the Things I Know* and a pen.

"Hmm? Oh, right," he said seeing the book. "What's your name?"

"Jim . . . " I muttered nervously.

"Gil?" Al asked.

"No . . . Jim. J-I-M." And then, suddenly, my courage returned. "Actually, you may hear from me again. I just found out I'm getting my book published."

"Really?" Al looked up, clearly interested as he handed me back the autographed book. "What's it about?"

"Well, I used to be a dittohead, but now, thanks in no small part to you, I'm a Democrat."

"Really? That's great! What can I tell Mark Luther?" In case you don't know, Al has a childhood buddy named Mark Luther, who is a dittohead. Al has him on his show occasionally, and he'll play a clip of Rush, and while he explains why it's a lie, in true dittohead fashion, Mark always refutes what Al says, continuing to believe in Rush's "Big Picture" (even though he acknowledges that Rush gets a lot of the little points wrong).

What I wanted to say to Al was: "At some point as a dittohead, I realized that those 'little points' that Rush gets wrong are the nails upon which the Big Picture hangs. A picture's no good if you don't have any nails to hang it on. In February of 2004, I ran out of nails." Yeah . . . that would've been cool!

What I actually said to Al was: "Well . . . um . . . You have to be ready to hear it . . . but . . . " And that was it. (It was early, I was tired and Al had a great-looking breakfast in front of him, which made me hungry.)

"Well, I'm sure your book will be great," Al said earnestly. "I'm looking forward to seeing it." I laughed, thanked him and tried to get out of there with what little dignity I could salvage.

The essence of treppenwitz is, "If I only knew then what I know now." This applies to my former life as a dittohead. There are lots of things I should have said or done, but they didn't occur to me at the time. There were lots of questions I should have asked, or facts I should have checked, but didn't.

Luckily, it wasn't too late for me, and hopefully it won't be too late for others. If you have a dittohead friend, maybe something you read here will help you to talk to them. If you are a dittohead, maybe something that you read here will resonate. Or maybe, just maybe, something in here will have changed your mind. If that's the case, then I will have gone a long way toward atoning for the sins of my past. I ask that you consider this book as my personal Hail Mary.

NOTES

•

2 : WHAT'S WITH ALL THE HATE?

1. Barbara and David Mikkelson, "The Clinton Body Count," *Urban Legend Reference Pages*, 24 January 2001, posted at http://www.snopes.com/inboxer/outrage/clinton.htm

5 : WATCHING THEM MAKE SAUSAGE

1. Robert E. Pierre, "Botched Name Purge Denied Some the Right to Vote," *The Washington Post*, 31 May 2001, P. A01.

7 : IRAQ—MY PERSONAL ROAD TO DAMASCUS

1. Britt Hume, "'Sexed Up' Claims Knocked Down," *Fox News*, 27 August 2003 posted at http://www.foxnews.com/story/0,2933,95850,00.html

8 : FROM HANNITY TO HUMANITY

1. Center For American Progress, "The Document Sean Hannity Doesn't Want You to Read," 16 June 2004 posted at http://www.americanprogress.org/site/pp.asp?c=biJRJ8OVF&b=91585

9 : THE DEATH OF FISCAL CONSERVATISM

1. Andrew Olivastro, "Issues 2002: Tax Reform for Economic Growth," The Heritage Foundation, 25 October 2002 posted at http://www. heritage.org/Research/Taxes/wm162.cfm

2. Congressional Budget Office, *Historical Budget Data*, "Revenues, Outlays, Deficits, Surpluses, and Debt Held by the Public, 1962 to 2004, Table 1" posted at http://www.cbo.gov/showdoc.cfm?index=1821&sequence=0#table1

3. U.S. Department of Commerce, Bureau of Economic Analysis, "National Income and Product Accounts Table

Table 1.1.5. Gross Domestic Product," Posted at http://www.bea.gov/bea/dn/nipaweb/TableView.asp#Mid

4. Congressional Budget Office, "Effective Tax Rates: 1979-2001, Table 1A" posted at http://www.cbo.gov/showdoc.cfm?index=5324&sequence=0#table1A

5. Congressional Budget Office, *Historical Budget Data*, "Revenues, Outlays, Deficits, Surpluses, and Debt Held by the Public, 1962 to 2004, Table 1" posted at http://www.cbo.gov/showdoc.cfm?index=1821&sequence=0#table1

6. Ibid.

7. U.S. Bureau of Economic Analysis, and Econstats, *National Income and Product Accounts (NIPA)*, "Table 1.1.1. Percent Change From Preceding Period in Real Gross Domestic Product," 5 August 2004, posted at http://www.econstats.com/nipa/NIPA1_1_1_.htm

11 : YOU CAN LEAD A DITTOHEAD TO KNOWLEDGE, BUT YOU CAN'T MAKE HIM THINK

1. The PIPA/Knowledge Network Polls, *The Separate Realities of Bush and Kerry Supporters*, "Perceptions of Pre-War Iraq: WMD," p. 3, 21 October 2004, posted at http://www.pipa.org/OnlineReports/Iraq/IraqRealities_Oct04/IraqRealities%20Oct04%20rpt.pdf

2. The PIPA/Knowledge Network Polls, *The Separate Realities of Bush and Kerry Supporters*, "Perceptions of Duelfer Report," p. 4, 21 October 2004, posted at http://www.pipa.org/OnlineReports/Iraq/IraqRealities_Oct04/IraqRealities%20Oct04%20rpt.pdf

3. The PIPA/Knowledge Network Polls, *The Separate Realities of Bush and Kerry Supporters*, "Iraq and Support for Al Queda," p. 5, 21 October 2004, posted at http://www.pipa.org/OnlineReports/Iraq/IraqRealities_Oct04/IraqRealities%20Oct04%20rpt.pdf

4. The PIPA/Knowledge Network Polls, *The Separate Realities of Bush and Kerry Supporters*, "Perceptions of Conclusion of 9/11 Commission Report on Iraq " p. 6, 21 October 2004, posted at http://www.pipa.org/OnlineReports/Iraq/IraqRealities_Oct04/IraqRealities%20Oct04%20rpt.pdf

5. The PIPA/Knowledge Network Polls, *The Separate Realities of Bush and Kerry Supporters*, "If No Pre-War Iraq WMD or Al Qaeda Support," p. 10, 21 October 2004, posted at http://www.pipa.org/OnlineReports/Iraq/IraqRealities_ Oct04/IraqRealities%20Oct04%20rpt.pdf

13 : SILENCING THE BIG GUN OF PERSONAL RESPONSIBILITY

1. Richard Gehr, "Mouth At Work: 'I'll tell you everything you need to know,' says Rush Limbaugh 'You need never read a newspaper again. I'll read them for you and tell you what to think.'" *Newsday*, 8 October 1990.

2. Jeff Cohen and Steve Rendell, "Limbaugh. A Color Man Who Has A Problem With Color?" *FAIR: Fairness and Accuracy in Reporting*. Posted at http://www.fair.org/index.php?page=2549

3. Republican National Committee, "RNC Chairman Ken Mehlman's Remarks Today At The NAACP National Convention," 14 July 2005. Posted at http://www.rnc.org/News/Read.aspx?ID=5631

4. Media Matters for America, "Limbaugh blasted Mehlman's renunciation of GOP racial tactics: 'Republicans are going to go bend over and grab the ankles'" 14 July 2005. Posted at http://mediamatters.org/items/200507140004

5. Ann Coulter, "The New and Improved Racism." 8 December 2004 Posted at http://www.anncoulter.org/columns/2004/120804.htm

6. Associated Press, "Radio Host Won't Take Back Rice Remarks." 19 November 2004. Posted at http://www.newsmax.com/archives/ic/2004/11/19/201237.shtml

7. NBC 4 News, "Conservative Host Pulled Off Air After Racial Slur." 9 November 2004. Posted at http://www.nbc4.tv/news/3901946/detail.html

8. Ann Coulter, "The New and Improved Racism." 8 December 2004 Posted at http://www.anncoulter.org/columns/2004/120804.htm

16 : BEATING THE GAY DRUMHEAD

1. Pam Belluck, "To Avoid Divorce, Move To Massachusetts," *The New York Times*, 14 November 2004, P.12. Statistics that this article are based on are from National Vital Statistics Reports. "Births, Marriages, Divorces, and Deaths: Provisional Data for 2003," 52 (22), 10 June 2004. Posted at http://www.cdc.gov/nchs/data/nvsr/nvsr52/nvsr52_22.pdf

2. Lara Jakes Jordan, "Santorum says homosexual acts are threat to American family," Associated Press, 22 April 2003. (Subscription only.) Text of Santorum's remarks available at multiple sites, including http://www.newyorker.com/talk/content/?030505ta_talk_hertzberg

3. U.S. Department of Health and Human Services, *Child Welfare Outcomes 2002: Annual Report.*

4. Abortion Statistics—World—U.S.—Demographics—Reasons. Posted at http://womensissues.about.com/cs/abortionstats/a/aaabortionstats.htm

17 : THE RODNEY DANGERFIELD OF ISSUES

1. Leonie Haimson, Michael Oppenheimer and David Wilcove, *The Way Things Really Are: Debunking Rush Limbaugh on the Environment.* Posted at http://www.environmentaldefense.org/documents/2432_WayThingsReallyAre.pdf

18 : THE WHOLE MADE-UP SOCIAL SECURITY THING

1. Social Security Administration, *SSA FY 1998 Accountability Report.* "Poverty Rate Among the Elderly," P.2 Posted at http://www.ssa.gov/finance/98md&a1.pdf

2. Carmen DeNavas-Witt, Bernadette D. Proctor, Robert J. Mills, U.S. Census Bureau, Current Population Reports, P60-226, *Income, Poverty and Health Insurance Coverage in the United States: 2003,* U.S. Government Printing Office, Washington D.C., 2004. Posted at http://www.census.gov/prod/2004pubs/p60-226.pdf

19 : TAXES ARE EVIL

1. The Rush Limbaugh Show, "The Top 50% pay 96.54% of All Income Taxes," 4 October 2005. Posted at http://www.rushlimbaugh.com/home/menu/cy2003.guest.html

20 : DITTOHEAD JUDICIAL PHILOSOPHY: CONSISTENTLY INCONSISTENT

1. Paul Gewirtz and Chad Golder, "So Who Are the Activists?" *New York Times*, Section A, Page 19, 6 July 2005.

21 : WHY TORTURE MATTERS

1. Lisa Porteus, "Gitmo Detainee Allegations Cause Uproar," 14 June 2005. Posted at http://www.foxnews.com/story/0,2933,159428,00.html

2. Associated Press, "Three Guantanamo Bay Detainees are Released," 22 August 2005. Posted at http://www.foxnews.com/story/0,2933,166460,00.html

3. "FBI Document," Posted at http://www.aclu.org/torturefoia/released/010505.html

4. Ibid.

22 : THEY ARE THE PARTY OF THE MILITARY. WE ARE THE PARTY OF THE TROOPS

1. R.G. Ratcliffe, "Bush Toughens His Stance on NATO Bombing," *Houston Chronicle*, Section A, P. 3, 9 April 1999. Posted at http://www.chron.com/CDA/archives/archive.mpl?id=1999_3130187

23 : THE LOG IN RUSH LIMBAUGH'S EYE

1. Media Matters for America, "Limbaugh Claimed his Abu Ghraib Comments 'Represent the Views of the Average American Leftist,'" 10 November 2005. Posted at http://mediamatters.org/items/200511100009

2. Ibid.

3. The Drudge Report, 14 September 2004. Posted at http://www.drudgereportarchives.com/data/2004/09/14/20040914_225202_bushtang.htm

4. The Rush Limbaugh Show, "Why Dan Rather's Out to Get Bush," 16 September 2004. Posted at http://www.rushlimbaugh.com/home/eibessential3/why_dan_rather_s_out_to_get_bush.guest.html